Cubase SX/SL

Tips and Tricks

Keith Gemmell

PC Publishing

PC Publishing
Keeper's House
Merton
Thetford
Norfolk IP25 6QH
UK

Tel 01953 889900
Fax 01953 889901
email info@pc-publishing.com
web site http://www.pc-publishing.com

First published 2004

ISBN 1870775 90 2

British Library Cataloguing in Publication Data
A catalogue record for this book is available from the British Library

Printed and bound in Great Britain by Biddles, Guildford

Introduction

Are you getting the best possible results from Cubase SX/SL? It's certainly one of the most powerful audio and MIDI production suites you can buy. But it's also a very large program with hundreds of features lurking deep beneath the surface. For this reason Cubase sometimes baffles even the most seasoned audio professionals, let alone the inexperienced user. After all, the Operation Manual is 828 pages long.

However, don't worry because this book is certainly not a another manual. It was written with the sole purpose of helping you get the most from Cubase with hints, tips and tricks on the many different aspects of using it creatively. In fact it's the kind of book you can pick up and dip in to, at anytime, on any particular subject area that happens to interest you – audio recording, MIDI recording, using specific editors and so on. Of course, to really get the most from the book, you're recommended to read it from cover to cover.

Cubase has arguably reigned supreme among sequencers for the best part of 14 years and its popularity shows no sign of abating as it continues to attract hordes of devoted users.

Looking back, it's easy to understand why. 1991 saw the introduction of Cubase Audio, the first sequencer to combine MIDI and audio recording. In 1996 Cubase VST, the first software studio with real-time EQ, effects, mixing and automation, was born. And – they're taken for granted now – in 1999 VST Instruments completely revolutionised the world of audio production. Eventually, with all the add-ons over the years, Cubase VST became rather unwieldy and in 2002 Steinberg replaced it with a much streamlined Cubase SX. This wasn't just another update but a completely new program based on Nuendo, Steinberg's already popular pro audio application.

Although well received there were some initial grumbles among the faithful about certain features being dropped from the program. Most were MIDI related and to be fair, the excellent MIDI plug-ins that appeared with SX 1.0 went some way to redress the loss. But now SX 2.0 has arrived, sporting a host of new features – a brand new VST 2.3 audio engine, Freeze function for VSTi's, Stacked Recording mode and a freely configurable user interface. What's more, if you're a loyal Cubase 5 user who didn't upgrade when the first version of SX was released, you should consider going for it now, because most of the features dropped from the program are back.

This book covers both releases of Cubase SX. Where there are differences you'll find them clearly marked. The program is also cross platform and available to both Windows and Mac users. Again, any differences are indicated. SX and SL also differ slightly and whenever something is specific to SX only it's marked accordingly.

Okay, let the tipping commence!

Contents

1 **Setup tips** *1*

2 **Working methods** *7*

3 **Project window tips** *21*

4 **Mixer tips** *37*

5 **Audio recording tips** *45*

6 **MIDI recording tips** *59*

7 **Time and tempo tips** *73*

8 **Inspector tips** *83*

9 **Key Editor tips** *91*

10 **List Editor tips** *101*

11 **Score Editor tips** *105*

12 **Drum track tips** *115*

13 **Logical Editor tips** *123*

14 **Audio tips** *129*

15 **Quantize tips** *137*

16 **Loops and hitpoints** *141*

Appendix 1: Default key commands *145*

Appendix 2: Tools summary *148*

Appendix 3: Useful contacts *151*

Index *153*

Setup tips

First and foremost

If you can afford it, invest in a computer that's been specially set up for audio. While making music on a computer may be very important to you, it's definitely not on the average computer manufacturer's priority list. Most PCs are built for light office use and are totally unsuitable for music studio work. In fact. audio recording is one of the most complicated, processor-intensive tasks you can ask a computer to do, so make sure your machine is up to the job. Figure 1.1 shows a PC set-up from Carillon Systems called the SL Project Studio with Edirol audio and MIDI interfaces.

Here are a few reputable companies that specialise in audio PCs:

- Andertons Music: www.andertonsonline.co.uk
- Carillon Audio Systems: www.carillondirect.com
- Digital Village: www.dv247.com
- Millennium Music: www.millennium-music.biz
- Philip Rees: www.philrees.co.uk

Figure 1.1
Carillon's SL Project Studio

Speed matters

Buy the fastest computer you can afford for the following reasons:

- You'll have more audio tracks to work with.
- You'll be able to use more effects and EQ.
- You'll be able to use more VST Instruments and plug-ins.

Windows 2000/XP and Cubase

Steinberg have optimised Cubase SX/SL for use with Windows 2000 and XP. However, from version 1.02 onwards you can also install Cubase SX/SL on Windows 98. This was an afterthought by Steinberg and was provided mainly for Cubase 5 users who wanted to try out the demo version of SX on their existing Windows 98 systems. But Steinberg don't provide any support for it, so if you're serious about Cubase SX/SL, install Windows 2000 or XP.

Windows 2000 and XP provide a reliable operating system for audio and MIDI but they do need optimising for use with Cubase SX/SL. Unfortunately these systems use something called ACPI mode (Automatic Power and Configuration Interface), which can lead to various problems with drivers and hardware, and in turn, your audio and MIDI applications. Depending on how serious the problem, you may need to either deactivate ACPI mode, or get rid of it completely by reinstalling the operating system.

The whole reinstallation and optimisation process is too much to include here but fortunately Steinberg have supplied it online at their web site - www.steinberg.net. Follow the Support > Knowledgebase links.

Mac OSX and Cubase

If you're a Mac owner, you'll need OSX version 10.2.5 and higher. G4 and G5 owners should not have a problem but if you have a G3 and OS X (10.2) runs slow on it, check that the graphics card in your machine supports Quartz Extreme, the 'composite windowing system' of Mac OS X, introduced with Jaguar (10.2).

Who's driving

PC version: Most audio hardware is supplied with a specially written ASIO driver and if you have one, that should be your first choice. If you haven't, use either the ASIO DirectX or the ASIO Multimedia driver, in that order, for better latency figures, Figure 1.2.

Mac version: OSX saw the introduction of Core Audio, and if your hardware has drivers specifically written for it they'll work fine and probably produce very low latency figures. However if your hardware has ASIO drivers, Steinberg strongly recommend that you use them as a first choice, Figure 1.3.

Quick tip

If you are doing a lot of audio recording consider adding a second, dedicated audio drive.

Info

SX 2 is a cross platform program. Open the box and you'll find two CDs, one for Windows, the other for Mac. Ten out of ten for this – now you can transfer your projects between a Mac and PC whenever you fancy.

Info

ASIO – Audio Stream In/Out technology is a software interface which communicates between music software, like Cubase SX and hardware, like your sound card.

Quick tip

Check your audio hardware manufacturer's site on a regular basis and download the latest drivers for your sound card.

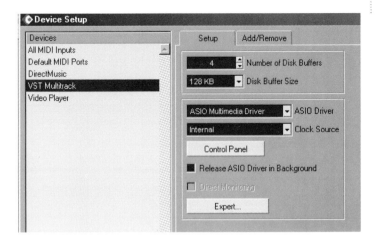

Figure 1.2
ASIO drivers are selected in the Device Setup
(VST Multitrack window)

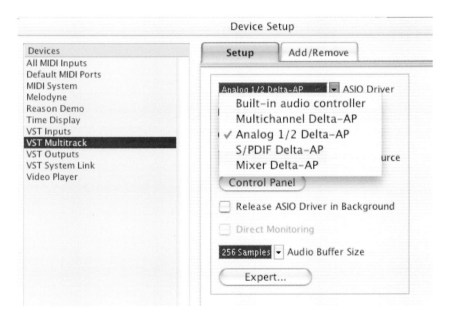

Figure 1.3
On the Mac, ASIO drivers are selected in the
Device Setup (VST Multitrack window)

Setting the buffer size

Buffers handle the flow of audio to and from the audio hardware. Their size affects the latency figures and audio performance. Basically, small buffer sizes mean lower latency. However, small buffer sizes also means poorer audio performance. So it's a matter of balance. Be prepared to experiment until you find the best settings for your particular hardware set-up.

On the PC, you can adjust the buffer settings in the ASIO Multimedia Setup - Advanced Options, Figure 1.4 (Device Setup > VST Multitrack page > click on the Control Panel button). Click on the Detect Buffer Size option and Cubase will automatically check for the ideal size and adjust it for you.

On the Mac, you can adjust the buffer settings in the VST Multitrack page (Devices > Device Setup), Figure 1.5.

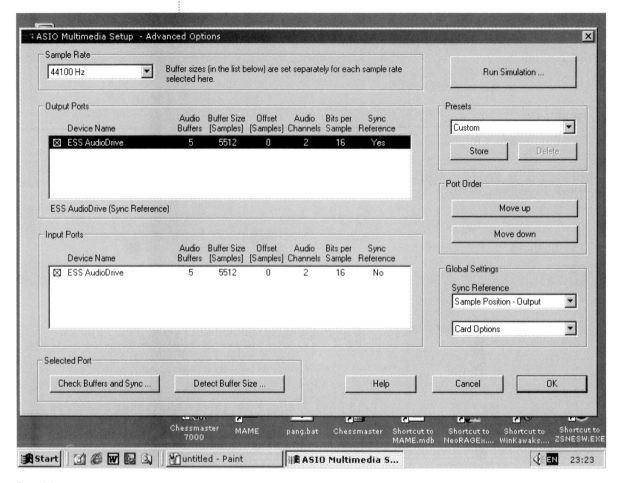

Figure 1.4
On the PC, adjust the buffer settings in the
ASIO Multimedia Setup - Advanced Options

Figure 1.5
On the Mac, adjust the buffer settings in the
VST Multitrack page (Devices > Device
Setup)

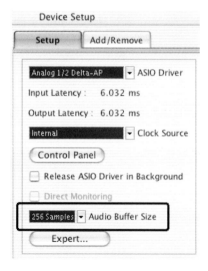

Setting the Sync Reference

On the PC, if you have more than one audio device, you'll need to select one as a Sync Reference. In the ASIO Multimedia Setup – Advanced Options, select the relevant device and move it to the top of the list.

Global settings

MIDI and audio playback is synchronised in the ASIO Multimedia Setup - Advanced Options (Global Settings section). For best results select Sample Position from the pop-up menu. If your card doesn't support Sample Position use DMA Block and use the Detect Buffer Size and Check Buffers and Sync options before you close the window.

Become an expert

If you've got problems with audio playback, press the Expert button, in the Device Setup, to reveal the Expert Settings page. Unless you're using a computer with more than one CPU the Multi Processing button will be disabled, Figure 1.6.

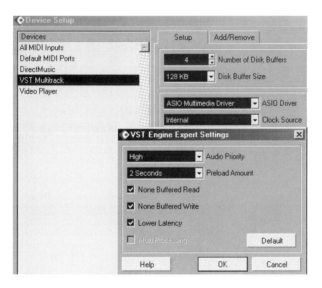

Figure 1.6
Expert settings

Information on the various settings found here can be found in the online help and may well solve your particular problem. Again it's a matter of experimenting. If you get in a mess, just click the Default button.

Quick tip

Cubase SX/SL is updated regularly so check www.steinberg.net on a regular basis and download the latest versions and bug fixes. Follow the Support > Knowledgebase links if you're having problems.

Quick tip

If you're having problems, read the 'Setting up your system' chapter in the Getting Started book that came with your copy of Cubase SX/SL - it's all there!

Working methods

Manual work

Obviously you're going to be referring to the SX/SL documentation from time to time, but let's face it, PDF documents are a pain. On-screen reading is okay for a while but quickly becomes tiresome. Printing the whole damn thing is time consuming and expensive, even in black and white. However, the Getting Started paperback, supplied with the program is excellent. So, tip number one – read it, from cover to cover. If you're new to Cubase and MIDI and audio sequencing the five tutorials will teach you the basics of recording, mixing, editing and using VST Instruments. The real nitty-gritty stuff though is to be found in the operation manual, supplied as – yes, you've guessed it – a PDF document. Read this too, if you have the time.

Conduct a search

Although the operation manual has an excellent index it doesn't always turn up exactly what you're looking for. Fortunately, an alternative version of the manual is duplicated as online help – HTML Help on the PC and via the Help Viewer on the Mac. Both have a search function so if you're stuck mid project, type in one or two words and up pops the relevant reading matter.

If you're using the PDF manual you can use the search facility built into Adobe Reader 6.0. Whole words and case sensitive options are available and you can even widen the search to the Internet. Adobe Reader uses Google to search for PDF documents. Just typing the words 'Cubase SX' will turn up all manner of useful stuff.

Any preferences?

Everybody has different ways of working. You may prefer your 'part' backgrounds to have a pretty colour – pink maybe, with the events and waveforms displaying black. Another person may prefer the opposite – events and waveforms displayed in pink against a grey background. Another might like transparent 'parts' (seems a bit pointless, but there you go).

So how do you get Cubase working just how you want it? Go to File > Preferences (on the Mac Cubase SX > Preferences) and use the dialogue boxes to tailor the program to suit your particular working methods. Any changes you make are saved and loaded when you next boot-up the program.

Appearances matter

Version 2 has an extra Appearance page in the Preferences, Figure 2.1. If you've upgraded from v.1 to v.2, the first thing you'll notice is the brand new look. As well as a choice of four skins you can adjust the brightness of the Project window events and the grid intensity in the Edit windows. A closer look around reveals a more ergonomic approach to detail with raised buttons and simplified icons throughout.

Figure 2.1
Use the Appearance page (Preferences) to customise the look of Cubase

Also new in the v.2 Preferences is the ability to rename, save and store Preferences presets for later recall. Different projects can now have different Preferences.

Start it up

On booting-up the program you may encounter a blank screen by default. To alter this behaviour go to Preferences > General (in v.1, Preferences > User Interface) and choose an option from the On Startup pop-up menu, Figure 2.2. Several alternatives are offered but perhaps the most useful is 'Show Open Options'. This provides a choice of recently used projects, a button to open other unlisted projects and a button to open a new project.

Another useful option is 'Open Default Project'. Of course you've got to save a new default project first. To do this, set up a project, just how you like it, and use 'File > Save As' to save it with the name 'default.cpr'. This feature is similar to the Autoload Song that appeared in earlier versions of Cubase.

Important note

Mac OSX users, be sure to type the .cpr extension when saving the 'default.cpr' file. Under normal circumstances, leaving this out is okay, but not this time!

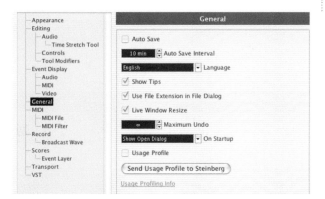

Figure 2.2
Cubase SX 2.0.1 Preferences, General page

Working templates

Choosing File > New Project presents a choice of templates which make good prac-
tical starting points for a number of potential projects. However, you may need a
more personal configuration. So, why not make your own? Your customised templates can be as elaborate as you want, containing VST Instruments, audio events
and so on – just like regular projects in fact. Save your template using File > Save
As Template…, Figure 2.3. You'll be prompted to enter a name before saving. To
open your new template, go to File > New Project and it will appear along side the
others in the list, Figure 2.4.

Quick tip

You can save any project as a
template. However, if you decide to
save just the track configuration,
ensure the audio clips are removed
from the Pool first.

Figure 2.3
Saving a template

Figure 2.4
Opening a template

Tool up

You can customise your own toolset in v.2 by Control-Clicking anywhere on the Toolbar and choosing what you want to see. This is useful because you may need quick access to different tools in different projects. Quite a few new tools are available and precisely which items you can and cannot customise depends on which editor you are using, Figure 2.5.

Figure 2.5
Control Click on the toolbar to customise your toolset

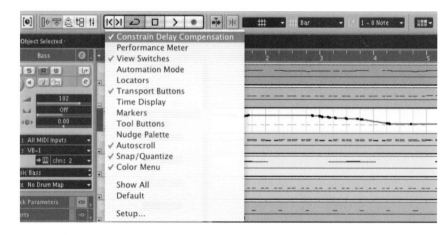

Select tools quickly, in the Project window, by using the keys 1 – 10 (left to right) on the alphanumeric part of your computer keyboard. F10 selects the next tool and F9 the previous one. Another way: right click in the grid area (on the Mac, Control Click) to access the Quick Menu (v.1), Figure 2.5. For a list of the tools and what they do, see the Appendix on page?

When version 1 appeared, Internet newsgroups and forums were awash with complaints about the missing toolbox, opened by right clicking in an editor. A round of applause please, because it's back in v.2, Figure 2.6. But if you don't happen to like it there's also a preference setting (Editor page) which gives you the Quick Menu instead.

Figure 2.6
Right click on the grid for the Pop-up toolbox

First things first

Check out the Project Setup before you settle down to any serious work, particularly with audio. The Project Setup is where you set a sample rate, record format and file type for the project. Most settings here can be changed mid project but deciding upon a sample rate is best done beforehand. All the audio files in a project must conform to the same sample rate otherwise things will sound dreadfully wrong. Make a decision and stick to it.

Which file type? On a PC it's usual to choose Wave files (.WAV) and on a Mac, AIFF files (.AIFF). If you're recording live performances, which are likely to be very long, consider the Wave64 option (SX 2 only).

Quick tip

Press 1 repeatedly to scroll through the object selection options for the Arrow tool. Press 8 repeatedly to scroll through the drawing options for the Pencil tool (SX 1). Press 9 repeatedly to toggle between Play and Scrub.

And which format (bit depth)? If your hardware only has 16 bit inputs there's nothing to be gained by selecting 24 bit except larger files with the same audio quality. There's one exception to this – recording with inserted effects using SX 2 (see page 51). Of course, if your hardware supports it, by all means choose a higher resolution but bear in mind that higher resolutions result in larger audio files, thereby putting more strain on your computer.

Your own devices

There's a fair chance that you own one of the many MIDI controllable devices listed in the MIDI Device Manager, Figure 2.7. If so, use the tabs to install it. Doing so will enable you to select the device's presets in the Inspector, Figure 2.8. Maybe you own a GM or XG synth that's not on the list. Just select the generic GM or XG options and rename it.

Quick tip

If you're short on space, on the Toolbar and you need to add more tools, consider removing the main tool buttons because you can have them as a floating box anyway.

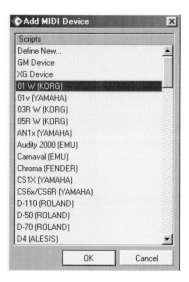

Figure 2.7 (left)
Installing The Korg 01 W using the MIDI Device Manager

Figure 2.8 (right)
The Korg 01 presets, shown in the Inspector

Quick tip

Use Devices > Show Panel to open a handy floating panel version of the Devices menu itself. This panel will float, whichever editing window you are using, giving you quick access to the Mixers, VST Instruments and so on, Figure 2.9.

Figure 2.9
Floating the Devices menu gains quick access to Mixers and so on

Renaming MIDI ports

Your MIDI inputs and outputs may have very long, unfriendly names. Why not give them a friendly nickname? Go to Device > Device Setup dialogue box, select the MIDI System device, and type a new name in the Setup section, Figure 2.10.

Figure 2.10
Give your MIDI devices friendly names in the Device Setup

Setup	Add/Remove		

Dir	Device	Active	Show
Out	FRED	No	Yes
Out	Delta–AP MIDI	Yes	Yes
In	Delta–AP MIDI	Yes	Yes
In	Delta–AP MIDI	Yes	Yes

MIDI Thru

You've set up your MIDI connections properly but you can't hear the sounds on your MIDI keyboard. 'MIDI in and out' is correctly set in the Inspector, you can see the 'MIDI in' activity (although not MIDI out) on the Transport panel but still no sound. What's wrong?

This is one of the most common problems asked by new users. It's most likely a MIDI Thru problem and easily solved by going to Preferences > MIDI and ticking the 'MIDI Thru Active' box. Cubase will now send the incoming MIDI data to the MIDI Out socket.

Most modern synthesisers have a backup facility whereby you can save its settings to disk, commonly known as a System Exclusive dump. You can do this using Cubase and record the 'dump' on a MIDI track.

Remote control

If you don't enjoy using a mouse to operate mixer faders and knobs you can purchase a remote control device such as a Tascam US-428 or Steinberg's Houston and use it to control Cubase SX/SL. To set it up, choose Generic Remote in the Device Setup and select the Add/Remove tab. After adding your particular device to the list, use the Setup tab to select it. Each device on the list has its own window with access to specific online help, Figure 2.11.

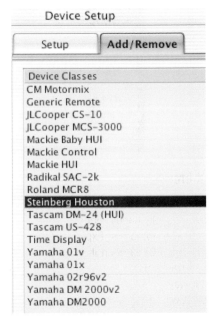

Device Setup

Setup	Add/Remove

Device Classes
CM Motormix
Generic Remote
JLCooper CS–10
JLCooper MCS–3000
Mackie Baby HUI
Mackie Control
Mackie HUI
Radikal SAC–2k
Roland MCR8
Steinberg Houston
Tascam DM–24 (HUI)
Tascam US–428
Time Display
Yamaha 01v
Yamaha 01x
Yamaha 02r96v2
Yamaha DM 2000v2
Yamaha DM2000

Figure 2.11
Installing remote control devices

Window layouts

A project is usually built in steps, something like: recording, MIDI editing, audio editing and mixing. Creating personal window layouts for the various tasks can make your work flow more efficiently. First, arrange the various windows needed for a particular task. Press W and up pops the Organise Layouts dialogue box Figure 2.12. Now you can create and name as many layouts as you need and remove those you don't. Check the 'Keep window open' option to leave the box floating, particularly if you need to switch between layouts frequently. If you change a layout it can be recaptured using Window > Window Layouts > Recapture Layout.

Quick tip

In the Window Layout box, double click in the number column to change layouts quickly.

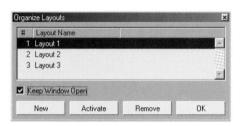

Figure 2.12
The Organise Layouts box

Window box

Despite the larger monitors available these days the computer screen soon becomes cluttered in Cubase SX. Add a few VST plug-ins to the already crowded view and things soon become confusing. You'll find it easier to manage the open windows with the Windows dialogue (Window > Windows…), Figure 2.13. In effect this replaces the first four items on the Window menu, enabling you to minimize, restore and close windows, all from one handy box. This box doesn't float so you'll have to close it before continuing work.

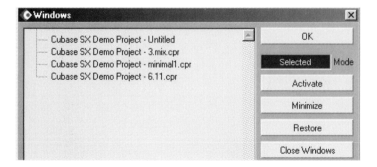

Figure 2.13
The Windows dialogue.

Just browsing

Have you found the Project Browser? A lot of people don't seem to notice its existence. It's jolly handy though and provides a list-based representation of a project, rather like Windows Explorer or OSX's Finder. Use Control+B (on the Mac, Command+B) to open it. From here you can view and numerically edit all events on all tracks using a value based list. That goes for automation too. In fact it's a great way of fine tuning track data after first entering it with the Pencil tool in the Project window – more precise and less clumsy, Figure 2.14.

Name	File	Start	End	Snap	Length	Offset	Volume
IP: 89bpm Sliced		1.01.01.000	2.01.01.000		1.0.0.0	0.0.0.0	
IP: 89bpm Sliced		2.01.01.000	3.01.01.000		1.0.0.0	0.0.0.0	
IP: 89bpm Sliced		3.01.01.000	4.01.01.000		1.0.0.0	0.0.0.0	
IP: 89bpm Sliced		4.01.01.000	5.01.01.000		1.0.0.0	0.0.0.0	
IP: 89bpm Sliced		5.01.01.000	6.01.01.000		1.0.0.0	0.0.0.0	
IP: 89bpm Sliced		6.01.01.000	7.01.01.000		1.0.0.0	0.0.0.0	
IP: 89bpm Sliced		7.01.01.000	8.01.01.000		1.0.0.0	0.0.0.0	
IP: 89bpm Sliced		8.01.01.000	9.01.01.000		1.0.0.0	0.0.0.0	
IP: 89bpm Sliced		9.01.01.000	10.01.01.000		1.0.0.0	0.0.0.0	
IP: 89bpm Sliced		10.01.01.000	11.01.01.000		1.0.0.0	0.0.0.0	
IP: 89bpm Sliced		11.01.01.000	12.01.01.000		1.0.0.0	0.0.0.0	
IP: 89bpm Sliced		12.01.01.000	13.01.01.000		1.0.0.0	0.0.0.0	
IP: 89bpm Sliced		13.01.01.000	14.01.01.000		1.0.0.0	0.0.0.0	
IP: 89bpm Sliced		14.01.01.000	15.01.01.000		1.0.0.0	0.0.0.0	
IP: 89bpm Sliced		15.01.01.000	16.01.01.000		1.0.0.0	0.0.0.0	
IP: 89bpm Sliced		16.01.01.000	17.01.01.000		1.0.0.0	0.0.0.0	
IP: 89bpm Sliced		17.01.01.000	18.01.01.000		1.0.0.0	0.0.0.0	
IP: 89bpm Sliced		18.01.01.000	19.01.01.000		1.0.0.0	0.0.0.0	
IP: 89bpm Sliced		19.01.01.000	20.01.01.000		1.0.0.0	0.0.0.0	
IP: 89bpm Sliced		20.01.01.000	21.01.01.000		1.0.0.0	0.0.0.0	
IP: 89bpm Sliced		21.01.01.000	22.01.01.000		1.0.0.0	0.0.0.0	
IP: 89bpm Sliced		22.01.01.000	23.01.01.000		1.0.0.0	0.0.0.0	
IP: 89bpm Sliced		23.01.01.000	24.01.01.000		1.0.0.0	0.0.0.0	
IP: 89bpm Sliced		24.01.01.000	25.01.01.000		1.0.0.0	0.0.0.0	

Figure 2.14
Use the Project Browser for detailed editing

Info

There's a list of default key commands in the Appendix.

Quick tip

To use key commands with plug-ins check the 'Plug-ins receive key commands' option in Preferences > VST (in v.1, Preferences > Editing).

Different strokes

There are key commands for most menus and dozens more for various functions. But remembering them all is a formidable task. You may find it easier to invent your own. Use the Key Commands dialogue to add yours and customise the existing ones. Version 2 saw the introduction of stored key commands, saved as presets for later recall. In other words: different key commands for different projects, Figure 2.15.

Here are a few of the most important key commands that you'll need.

Pad Enter	Play
Pad +	Fast Forward On/Off
Pad –	Rewind On/Off
Pad *	Record
Pad /	Cycle On/Off
Pad ,	Return to Zero
Pad 0	Stop
Pad 1	Go to Left Locator
Pad 2	Go to Right Locator

Figure 2.15
You can create and customise your own key commands

Enter to exit!

Often overlooked; to close down an Editor – press the Enter key.

Switch keys

Annoying isn't it when you might want to switch a Preference such as 'Enable Solo on Selected Track' on and off whilst you are working on a project? In v.1 you have to wade through the Preferences menu to do so. Not so in v.2. You can now assign Key Commands to toggle a whole bunch of switchable Preferences. A minute or two setting them up will save much frustration and unwelcome interruptions to your workflow.

Macro

If you have a multiple task to perform, such as selecting a group of audio events on a single track, creating a fade in and exporting them as an audio mix-down you can make light work of it by setting up a Macro in the Key Commands dialogue. A Macro is a set of commands which are performed one after another in one single pass.

Plug watch

Keep tabs on your VST Plug-ins with the help of the Plug-in Information window, found in the Devices menu Figure 2.16. Every installed plug-in will show up here. Press the Update button if you have recently installed one and you can't see it. Apart from specific plug-in information, you can see how many are currently in use and deactivate those you don't want on the menu.

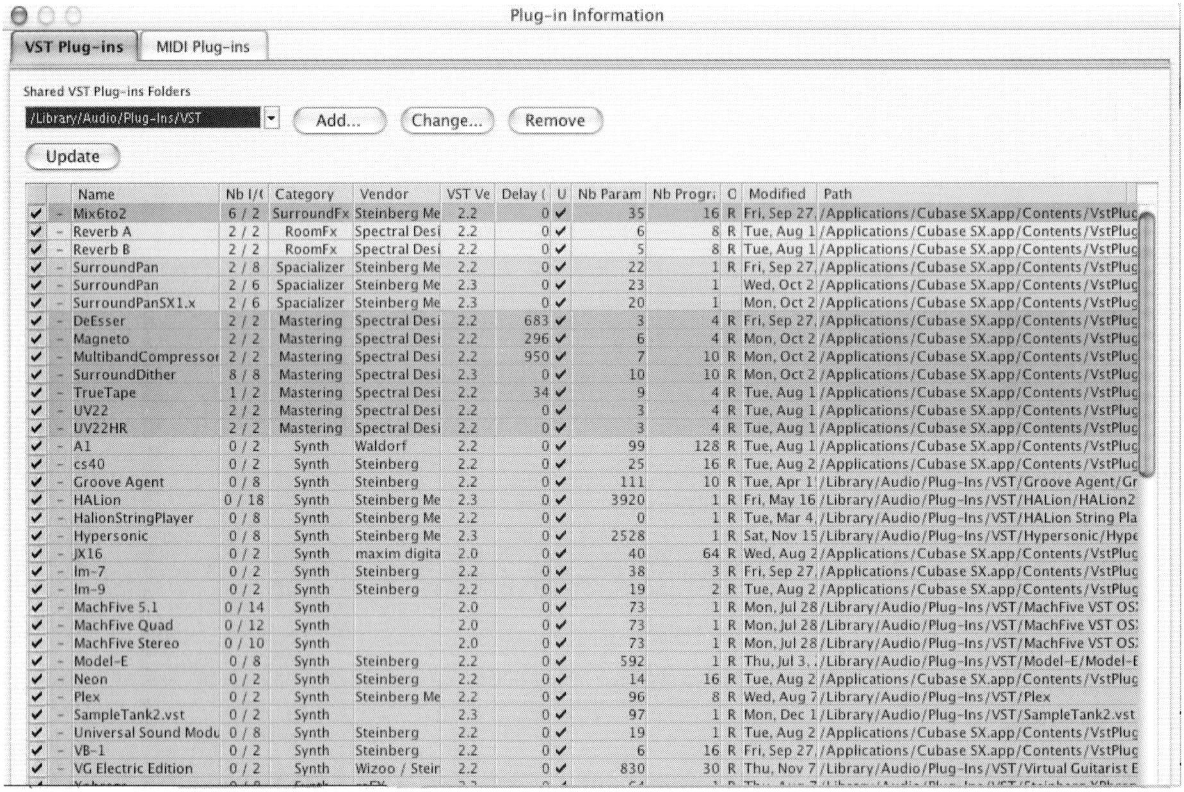

Figure 2.16
The Devices menu

Plug-in Information

VST Plug-ins　MIDI Plug-ins

Shared VST Plug-ins Folders
/Library/Audio/Plug-Ins/VST　▾　(Add...)　(Change...)　(Remove)

(Update)

Name	Nb I/(	Category	Vendor	VST Ve	Delay (	U	Nb Param	Nb Progr	O	Modified	Path
Mix6to2	6 / 2	SurroundFx	Steinberg Me	2.2	0	✔	35	16	R	Fri, Sep 27,	/Applications/Cubase SX.app/Contents/VstPlu
Reverb A	2 / 2	RoomFx	Spectral Desi	2.2	0	✔	6	8	R	Tue, Aug 1	/Applications/Cubase SX.app/Contents/VstPlu
Reverb B	2 / 2	RoomFx	Spectral Desi	2.2	0	✔	5	8	R	Tue, Aug 1	/Applications/Cubase SX.app/Contents/VstPlu
SurroundPan	2 / 8	Spacializer	Steinberg Me	2.2	0	✔	22	1	R	Fri, Sep 27,	/Applications/Cubase SX.app/Contents/VstPlu
SurroundPan	2 / 6	Spacializer	Steinberg Me	2.3	0	✔	23	1		Wed, Oct 2	/Applications/Cubase SX.app/Contents/VstPlu
SurroundPanSX1.x	2 / 6	Spacializer	Steinberg Me	2.3	0	✔	20	1		Mon, Oct 2	/Applications/Cubase SX.app/Contents/VstPlu
DeEsser	2 / 2	Mastering	Spectral Desi	2.2	683	✔	3	4	R	Fri, Sep 27,	/Applications/Cubase SX.app/Contents/VstPlu
Magneto	2 / 2	Mastering	Spectral Desi	2.2	296	✔	6	4	R	Mon, Oct 2	/Applications/Cubase SX.app/Contents/VstPlu
MultibandCompressor	2 / 2	Mastering	Spectral Desi	2.2	950	✔	7	10	R	Mon, Oct 2	/Applications/Cubase SX.app/Contents/VstPlu
SurroundDither	8 / 8	Mastering	Spectral Desi	2.3	0	✔	10	10	R	Mon, Oct 2	/Applications/Cubase SX.app/Contents/VstPlu
TrueTape	1 / 2	Mastering	Spectral Desi	2.2	34	✔	9	4	R	Tue, Aug 1	/Applications/Cubase SX.app/Contents/VstPlu
UV22	2 / 2	Mastering	Spectral Desi	2.2	0	✔	3	4	R	Tue, Aug 1	/Applications/Cubase SX.app/Contents/VstPlu
UV22HR	2 / 2	Mastering	Spectral Desi	2.2	0	✔	3	4	R	Tue, Aug 1	/Applications/Cubase SX.app/Contents/VstPlu
A1	0 / 2	Synth	Waldorf	2.2	0	✔	99	128	R	Tue, Aug 1	/Applications/Cubase SX.app/Contents/VstPlu
cs40	0 / 2	Synth	Steinberg	2.2	0	✔	25	16	R	Tue, Aug 2	/Applications/Cubase SX.app/Contents/VstPlu
Groove Agent	0 / 8	Synth	Steinberg	2.2	0	✔	111	10	R	Tue, Apr 1	/Library/Audio/Plug-Ins/VST/Groove Agent/Gr
HALion	0 / 18	Synth	Steinberg Me	2.3	0	✔	3920	1	R	Fri, May 16	/Library/Audio/Plug-Ins/VST/HALion/HALion2
HalionStringPlayer	0 / 8	Synth	Steinberg Me	2.2	0	✔	0	1	R	Tue, Mar 4,	/Library/Audio/Plug-Ins/VST/HALion String Pla
Hypersonic	0 / 8	Synth	Steinberg Me	2.3	0	✔	2528	1	R	Sat, Nov 15	/Library/Audio/Plug-Ins/VST/Hypersonic/Hype
JX16	0 / 2	Synth	maxim digita	2.0	0	✔	40	64	R	Wed, Aug 2	/Applications/Cubase SX.app/Contents/VstPlu
lm-7	0 / 2	Synth	Steinberg	2.2	0	✔	38	3	R	Fri, Sep 27,	/Applications/Cubase SX.app/Contents/VstPlu
lm-9	0 / 2	Synth	Steinberg	2.2	0	✔	19	2	R	Tue, Aug 2	/Applications/Cubase SX.app/Contents/VstPlu
MachFive 5.1	0 / 14	Synth		2.0	0	✔	73	1	R	Mon, Jul 28	/Library/Audio/Plug-Ins/VST/MachFive VST OS:
MachFive Quad	0 / 12	Synth		2.0	0	✔	73	1	R	Mon, Jul 28	/Library/Audio/Plug-Ins/VST/MachFive VST OS:
MachFive Stereo	0 / 10	Synth		2.0	0	✔	73	1	R	Mon, Jul 28	/Library/Audio/Plug-Ins/VST/MachFive VST OS:
Model-E	0 / 8	Synth	Steinberg	2.2	0	✔	592	1	R	Thu, Jul 3,	/Library/Audio/Plug-Ins/VST/Model-E/Model-E
Neon	0 / 2	Synth	Steinberg	2.2	0	✔	14	16	R	Tue, Aug 2	/Applications/Cubase SX.app/Contents/VstPlu
Plex	0 / 2	Synth	Steinberg Me	2.2	0	✔	96	8	R	Wed, Aug 7	/Library/Audio/Plug-Ins/VST/Plex
SampleTank2.vst	0 / 2	Synth		2.3	0	✔	97	1	R	Mon, Dec 1	/Library/Audio/Plug-Ins/VST/SampleTank2.vst
Universal Sound Modu	0 / 8	Synth	Steinberg	2.2	0	✔	19	1	R	Tue, Aug 2	/Applications/Cubase SX.app/Contents/VstPlu
VB-1	0 / 2	Synth	Steinberg	2.2	0	✔	6	16	R	Fri, Sep 27,	/Applications/Cubase SX.app/Contents/VstPlu
VG Electric Edition	0 / 2	Synth	Wizoo / Stein	2.2	0	✔	830	30	R	Thu, Nov 7	/Library/Audio/Plug-Ins/VST/Virtual Guitarist E

Regular savings

Save your projects regularly, as you go, using Control+S (on the Mac, Command+S). You know it makes sense. It not only saves the project, but a good deal of angst too, if your computer crashes.

Crossing platforms

If you're saving a project created on a Windows PC your files will open on a Mac. However, if you're creating a project on a Mac and you want it be compatible with both platforms, make sure that 'Use File Extension in File Dialog' is ticked in the Preferences General page (in v.1, User Interface page). When this is activated, the file extension '.cpr' will be added automatically each time you save it.

Backing up

Use the automatic back up system if you're forgetful. Go to Preferences > General (In v.1, Preferences > User Interface) and tick the Auto Save box. Specify a time interval for the operation. Any open files – your projects.bak – will be backed up at the specified interval in the project folder, as you work. Your original files are unchanged. If things go wrong and you want to go back, select 'Revert' from the File menu and you will be asked if you want to open the backup or the original file.

Archive back up

Before backing up a complete project to a CD use Pool > Prepare Archive… to tidy things up. Any stray audio files found outside the project folder will be returned to it. Use the Freeze Edit option and you will not need to save the Edit folder.

Opening files

If you're opening a project containing audio files archived on a CD, perhaps created on another platform, it's best to copy the entire folder onto your computer desktop before opening the project file. Otherwise audio files will not be referenced properly.

Importing audio

It's a good idea to have imported audio files copied into the project's audio folder and thereby referenced from there. This keeps things nice and tidy. Go to Preferences > Editing-Audio and select 'Open Options Dialog'. Now, when you import an audio file an Options dialogue will appear asking you if want to copy the file to the Audio folder and convert it to the Project settings. If you're using v.1, go to Preferences > Audio and choose 'Copy to Project Folder'. There are further options such as 'Copy and Covert'. This will convert the files to the same sample rate and size.

Cleaning up

Save valuable hard disk space and use the Cleanup function – File > Cleanup. Cubase will scan selected folders or entire hard disks for project folders containing wayward audio and image files that are not used by any project. These will be listed in a dialogue box awaiting your further action. Delete with extreme care. If you've used any of these audio files in other projects, or moved or renamed them without updating their paths Cubase will consider them unused.

Slide control

How do you like your knobs and sliders? Go to Preferences > Editing-Controls (In v.1, Preferences > User Interface – Controls). Here you can select your preferred ways of controlling knobs, sliders and value fields (Figure 2.17). For example, to

Quick tip

Back up files, with the extension '.bak', are deleted on closing the project so remember to save them first.

Quick tip

Using File > Recent Projects is often much quicker than trawling through layers of folders to find a project.

Info

You can't open Cubase 5 songs but you can import them, File > Import > Cubase Song… They are converted into project files but things will very likely be different. For details of how SX/SL handles older Cubase files look up Importing Older Cubase Files in the online help menu.

Info

Image and Fade files can be safely deleted using the Cleanup function because they will be recreated again on use.

Figure 2.17
Use Preferences menu to customise knobs and sliders

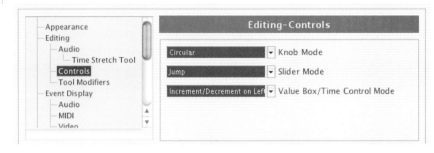

have the mouse scroll values on the Transport panel, fader style, choose 'Increment/Decrement on Left Click and Drag' in the pop up menu – very handy.

History lesson

We all make mistakes and change our minds. You can use Undo and Redo repeatedly to get back where you need to be but it's quicker to use the Edit History window (Figure 2.18). Use Edit > History to open it. All your actions are recorded here and recorded in a list, the most recent at the top. A shaded curtain can be dragged down, using a blue divider line, to cover anything that you wish to undo. If you want to redo things, simply drag the curtain back up to a convenient point. This window floats and the changes are reflected in the Project window instantly. It's not saved with the project though, so get things right before you close it down.

Figure 2.18
You can undo and redo all your actions in the Edit History window

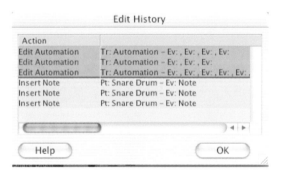

Handy Edit menu key commands

Undo: Ctrl+Z (on the Mac, Command+Z)
Redo: Shift+Ctrl+Z (on the Mac, Shift+Ctrl+Z)

Join the Library

It's very likely that you already store your favourite loops, samples and even video clips in various folders on your hard disk. Accessing them might be made easier by using the new Library feature (SX 2 only). You can create as many libraries as you need and drag and drop files directly into Cubase or use the Open Library and Save Library menu items. These files have the extension '.npl'.

Track exchange

You may need to exchange tracks with a friend or working partner who also uses SX or Nuendo. Or, you may want to save a particular track configuration for later use in your own projects. You can do this by using the Import and Export items on the File menu. All track related information – mixer channel settings, automation sub tracks and so on – will be saved in a separate 'media' folder and saved as an XML file.

Data dump

If you modify your synthesiser's presets, you can use Cubase to record and save the altered settings, along with your project data. It's a more convenient method than saving them to a floppy disk. For a start, everything is in one place – the project folder. Most synths and sound modules allow you transmit the settings. You'll probably find the information tucked away in the back of the manual. You know, where all the small print and technical jargon lies.

Before you make the dump go to Preferences > MIDI-Filter and un-tick the Sysex box in the Record section. Leave the Sysex box in the Filter section ticked.

The data is recorded in the usual way, on a MIDI track and is best placed in a silent bar at the beginning of the project. When you transmit the data back to the synth, make sure that it is correctly routed. Again, check the manual because the device may receive the data on a specific MIDI channel. When you've finished the dump open the List Editor and check that the data has actually been recorded, Figure 2.19. Click on the data itself, in the Comment column, if you're into editing System Exclusive data.

Info

System Exclusive dump – term commonly used for transmitting a device's System Exclusive data and recording it to a floppy or hard disk drive.

Figure 2.19
Data dump viewed in the List and MIDI SysEx Editors.

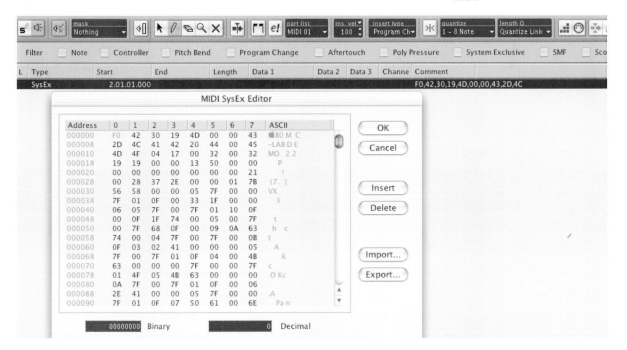

Jot it down

The Notepad in Cubase is easily overlooked but it's useful for jotting down all kinds of information about a project – song lyrics, song structure ideas, external equipment connections, in fact anything you think might be forgotten when you return to the project at a later date.

In version 2, an additional Notepad is available for each track. You'll find it in the Inspector. Use it to jot down information related to a specific track, Figure 2.20.

Figure 2.20
In SX 2, each track has its own Notepad

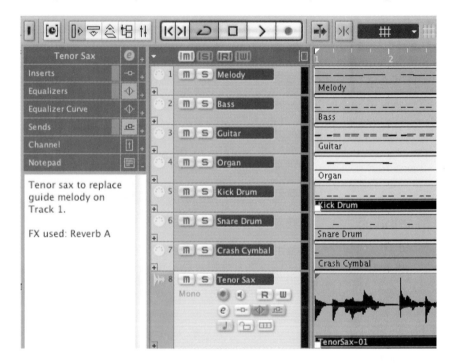

Choice editing

Which Editor do use the most? To have Cubase open the Editor of choice when you double click an event or part, go to Event Display-MIDI page in the Preferences dialogue and set it in the Default Edit Action menu.

Project window tips

Open windows

Having more than one Project Window opened at a time enables you to copy and paste data between arrangements. Select the events in one window, press Ctrl+C (on the Mac, Command+C), switch to the second window, position the Project Cursor at the right spot and press Ctrl+V (on the Mac, Command+V). Completely new versions of a tune can be restructured this way and easily compared by switching window views.

Take a shortcut

Speed up your workflow by making full use of the shortcuts provided on the Toolbar. There are six of them in v.1. From left to right:

- The first is the Active project indicator. It glows blue when a project is active (red in v.1).
- The second shows and hides the Inspector. The Inspector is very useful but it occupies valuable screen space. Turn it off when you want more events displayed.
- The third shows and hides the Info line. The Info line is often overlooked but in fact provides a very quick way of editing many events.
- The fourth shows and hides the Overview. A useful way of navigating around large projects but it takes up valuable space. Turn it off when not in use.
- The fifth opens the Pool.
- The sixth opens the Mixer.

Make it snappy

When audio events are moved with Snap activated, it isn't always the beginning of the event that is used as a reference. Audio events contain Snap Points which can be set in the Sample Editor, Figure 3.1. You can also set the Snap Point of an audio event directly in the Project Window:

> ### Quick tip
>
> Activate the Autoscroll button to have the Project cursor permanently visible. Tick 'Stationary Cursors' in the Transport Preferences and it will remain centre screen, as events scroll by.

> ### Quick tip
>
> For a thick Project cursor, change its width to '4' in the Transport Preferences.

Figure 3.1
The snap point appears as a thin blue line in the event.

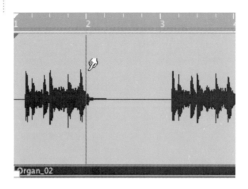

- Select the event.
- Place the Project Cursor at a chosen point within the event.
- Select 'Snap Point to Cursor' from the Audio menu and the Snap Point will be displayed as a blue line in the Project window.

Stay informed

Figure 3.2
Stay informed and use the Info line.

It's often said that knowledge is power. Well so is information! Keep an eye on the Info line. You can view and edit precise details about any selected event here,

Oversee events

Do you find it difficult to find far flung events in the Project window? Use the Project Overview Line to nip around, your Projects, Figure 3.3. All the events are shown as boxes. The blue rectangle is used to 'home in' on an area of the project. Resize the rectangle – drag the edges – to zoom in or out.

Figure 3.3
Use the Project Overview Line to move around Project

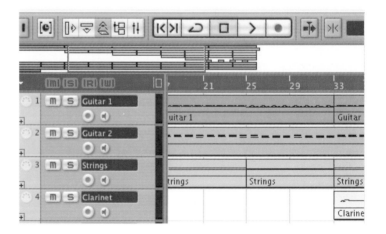

Breaking the rules

The display format chosen in the Project Setup appears on the Transport panel and the Ruler. However an independent display can be set for the Ruler. Click on the arrow button (far right of the ruler), and select an option from the pop-up menu. This is useful if you are working with video and need bars and beats on the Transport panel and a frame rate in the Ruler, Figure 3.4.

Making the rules

In version 2, a peek at the Add Track menu reveals two new track types – Ruler tracks and FX Channel tracks. You can add as many ruler tracks to a project as you like, and each one can show a separate display format: – Bars + Beats, Seconds, Time code and so on. All jolly useful because you can position them adjacent to relevant tracks by dragging them up or down in the Project window, Figure 3.5.

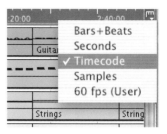

Figure 3.4
Choosing a Ruler display format

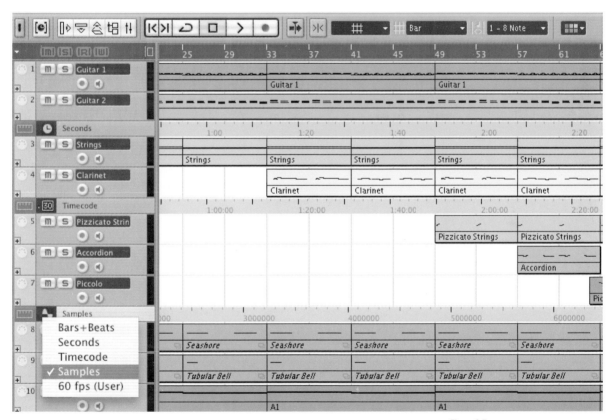

Figure 3.5
Three different Ruler tracks – Seconds, Timecode, Samples.

Zooming about

Lots of choice here. Apart from the comprehensive zoom options found in the Edit menu the horizontal and vertical sliders (bottom right) are very useful. The pop-up menus are often overlooked, Figure 3.6. Devise your own zoom option presets and add them to the menu using the dialogue box.

Figure 3.6
You can zoom in or out quickly using the Zoom pop-up menu

Handy zoom key commands

H – zoom in.
G – zoom out.
Shift+F – zoom to full project.
Shift+Zoom tool – zoom to full project.

Show for me

Figure3.7
Click on the arrow for the Track Controls Settings

You may prefer to work with a leaner Track Control list. To access the Track Controls Settings, click on the arrow in the top left corner of the Track list, Figure 3.7. You can hide items by moving them from the Used Controls list to the Available Controls list. Why would you want to do this? An example – if you're not using automation, Record/Write-Enable could be dispensed with, Figure 3.8.

Or, if the track is a purely conventional musical project, you could get rid of the button used for switching between Musical and Linear time base.

Another handy feature here is the facility to regroup the controls to various sets and number them 1, 2, 3 and so on. Now when you resize the Track list (see below) the grouped controls will remain together (providing the Wrap Controls box is ticked).

> **Quick tip**
>
> Double click in the empty space at the bottom of the track list to add a MIDI or audio track. Its type is determined by the last track already in the list.

Keeping track

You can extend MIDI or Audio Track Lists by dragging them to the right, across the screen. The further you go, the more information is revealed, Figure 3.9. Of course, this limits your working area in the event display, although hiding the Inspector will retrieve it (use the Show Inspector button). On the plus side, several Inspector settings are added to the list as well.

Figure 3.9
To extend the Track List, drag it to the right

Handy track key commands

Ctrl+down/up (on the Mac, Command+down/up) – to resize selected tracks.
Ctrl+click (on the Mac, Command+clicking) – to select multiple tracks.
Shift+click – to select a continuos range of tracks.

> **Quick tip**
>
> Press Ctrl (on the Mac, Command) and drag up or down to resize all the Project window tracks together. Activate 'Snap Track Heights' on the Track scale pop-up to change the track height in set increments.

Lock up

It's all to easy to accidentally move an event. To prevent this happening, lock the tracks. Click the Lock icon on the Track list or in the Inspector. To unlock it, click again.

> **Info**
>
> Exactly how the Lock function behaves is defined in the 'Lock Event Attributes' pop-up menu in the Preferences dialogue (Editing page).

Fol-de-ro-do

If you're working on a large project or just running out of screen space, consider using folder tracks, Project > Add Track > Folder. You can drag several tracks onto the Folder Track. A big band piece, for example, might have separate folders for saxes, trumpets and trombones, Figure 3.10. Need the four trumpets repeated at bar 33? No problem. Just copy and paste them all in one go. You can easily open and close folders for individual editing on the different parts.

Figure 3.10
Big band project with four Folder Tracks

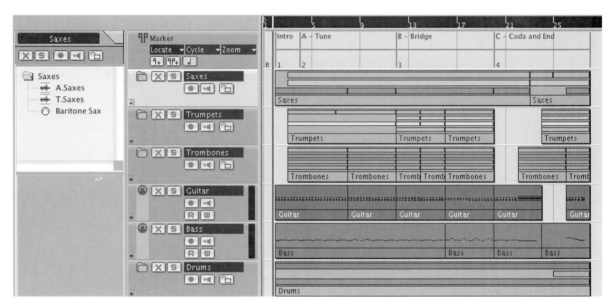

Auto fades

Having automatic fades activated will help smooth the transition between audio events. Apply it to a specific track by using the icon in the Inspector to open the Auto Fades dialogue Figure 3.11. Apply it to the project in general by using the Auto Fades Settings (Project menu). There's much to play with here in the form of fade curves and so on. However, there's a downside to all this. Because the fades are played back in real time and are not permanent, more processing power is used. Although a very useful feature, it's probably best used on a track basis rather than globally and only when necessary. Let your ears be the judge.

Shuffle along

A handy way to exchange event positions: select Shuffle from the Grid pop-up menu, Figure 3.12. Now, with Snap activated, you can change the order of adjacent events. For example, if you have two adjacent events and drag the first one to the right, past the second event, the two events will change places. It works the same way with more events and is very useful if you want to move an event forwards or backwards. The other events shuffle along and close the gap, Figure 3.13 and 3.14.

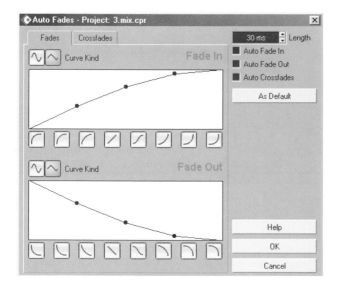

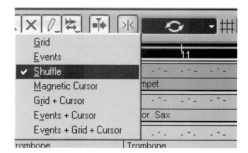

Figure 3.11 (left)
You can choose an automatic curve shape
and edit it

Figure 3.12
Selecting Shuffle from the Grid pop-up

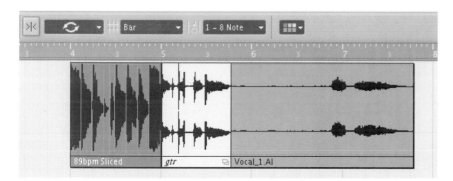

Figure 3.13
Events before shuffling

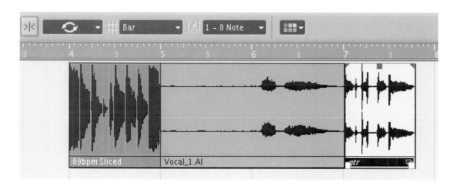

Figure 3.14
Events after shuffling

It's a drag

It's very easy to accidentally move an event when you select it with the mouse. If you find yourself doing this, use the variable Drag Delay setting in the Preferences > Editing page. It's set at 200 ms by default but 500 ms is safer. Mind you, it could irritate the more impatient user.

Under the Cursor

A handy way to quickly select events and parts: go to Preferences > Editing and check Auto Select events under Cursor. Now, select a track and as you move the Project Cursor everything under it is selected.

Share and share alike

A quick way to copy events – select them and use Ctrl+K (on the Mac, Command+K) or Edit > Repeat... If the Shared Copies option in the Repeat dialogue box is activated, and you are repeating audio or MIDI events, the new events will be shared copies of the original. If you edit the contents of a shared copy, all other shared copies of the same part are automatically edited in the same way. They're recognisable by italic text.

What a drag

There was much wailing and gnashing of teeth among the faithful when Cubase SX was found not to include the handy Alt-Click and drag feature, used for repeating events. Steinberg must have got the message because it has returned in v.2. Just select the event(s), press Alt (on the Mac, Option), grab the lower right corner – the mouse pointer changes to the Pencil tool – and drag as far as you need. The copies will follow. Figure 3.15.

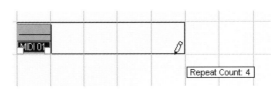

Figure 3.15
Repeating events with the Pencil tool

Use drag and drop

Although creating events is usually done by recording you can drag and drop material from the Desktop, the Pool, another open Project, the Audio Part Editor, and the Sample Editor. Get the habit and save time.

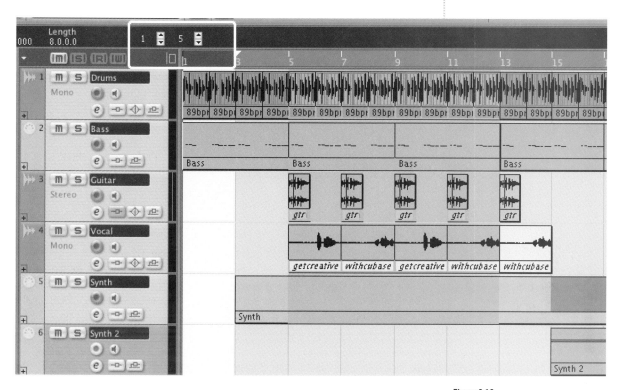

Figure 3.16
You can set a Range in the Info line (white rectangle)

Info

With the Range tool selected, you can set complete ranges and individual track ranges in the Info line as an alternative method to using the mouse. Detailed editing can also be performed there, Figure 3.16.

A Range of options

Project window editing isn't restricted to selecting whole events and parts with the Arrow tool; you can make selections with the Range tool as well. These are independent of the event, part and track boundaries. Once the Range tool is selected all the options from the Edit > Select menu become available as well as the Edit > Range menu. You can also cut, copy and paste Ranges in the normal way.

Quick tip

To duplicate a selected range, hold down Alt (on the Mac, Option) and drag.

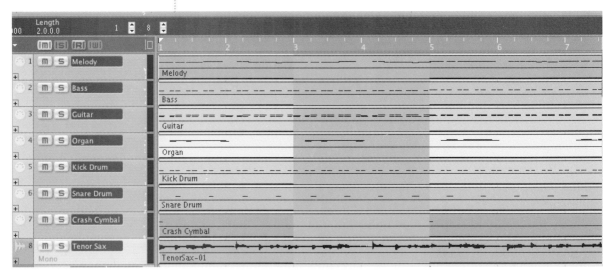

Figure 3.17
Before inserting two bars space

Figure 3.18
Two bars space inserted. All events to the right are moved along by two bars

Silence please

You've finished a piece and decided that it needs a bridge in the middle. Instead of going to work with the Scissors tool, splitting events on separate tracks, use the Range tool or the Locators. It's much quicker. Make a selection and press Shift+Ctrl+E (on the Mac, Shift+Command+E). Silence is inserted in the selected area and all the split events are moved to the right, making the arrangement that much longer, Figures 3.17 and 3.18.

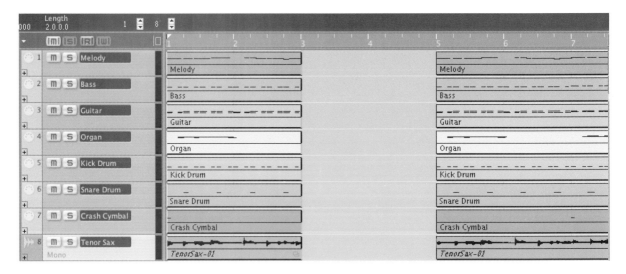

This is also useful for inserting space at the beginning of a project, to make way for MIDI file set-up data and so on. Repeating the the keystroke will move the whole project by the same amount each time.

Fast moves

Make full use of the Transport menu options to get around the Project menu quickly and easily.

Handy Locator key commands are:

P – send locators to selection.
L – locate a selection.
Alt (on the Mac, Option) – play a selected range.
Shift+G – loop a selection.

Follow me

Check 'Locate when Clicked in Empty Space' in the Transport Preferences, to do just that. Now click in an empty space and the Project Cursor will follow on.

Personal transport

A completely new Transport panel has been included with v.2 and opinions are likely to be divided on whether it's easier or more complicated to use. One thing's for sure, the default version is much larger and takes up extra screen space. As well as the usual things it now displays CPU Usage and Disk Cache Usage meters, Markers, audio input level meter and an output level control slider. However, just as in Cubase 5, you have the option to display cut down versions. There's a choice of six and you can also customise your own. Ctrl-Click anywhere on the Transport panel to bring up a menu of options, Figure 3.19.

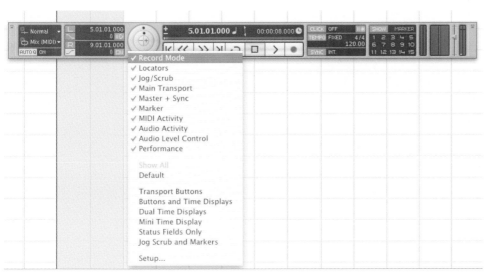

Info

You can adjust the width of the Project Cursor line in the Transport Preferences.

Quick tip

Double click in the Ruler to move the cursor and stop or start playback.

Figure 3,19
Transport panel options

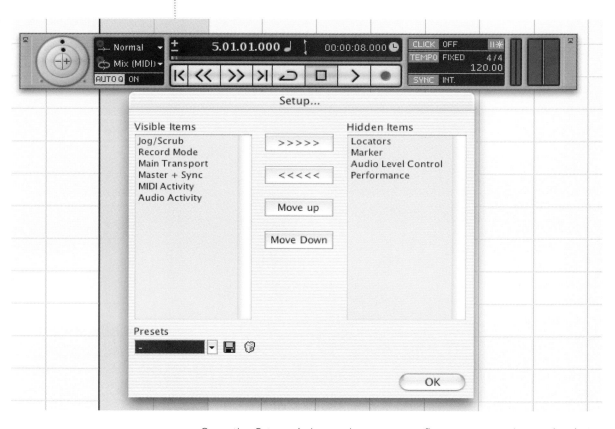

Open the Setup window and you can configure your own by moving items between the Visible and Hidden columns. A particularly neat feature here is the ability to reposition items on the Transport panel by altering their position in the Visible list, Figure 3.20. For example, if an item is at the top, it will be seen at the far left on the panel. Conversely, if it's at the bottom it will be positioned on the far right. Anywhere in-between and it will be positioned, of course, somewhere in-between. The changes are reflected immediately in the panel itself, so position the window so that you can see the Transport panel as you make the alterations.

Jogging along

Visually, the most striking thing about the new Transport bar is the addition of a large scrub dial (SX 2 only), Figure 3.21. You can use the outer wheel (Shuttle Speed control) to play the project at any speed, forwards or backwards, to quickly locate or 'cue' to a specific position in a project.

The inner one acts as a jog wheel. You use it to move the playback position manually, forwards or backwards – much like scrubbing on a tape deck. In the good old days of analogue recording, engineers would manually adjust the tape spools on a tape recorder. Whilst rotating the spools, backwards and forwards, they would listen intently, until exactly the right spot for editing could be heard before marking the tape and finally, splicing it with a razor blade. You can use the inner wheel in the same way, to pinpoint editing spots.

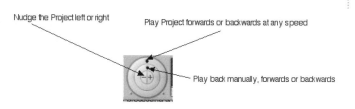

Nudge the Project left or right

Play Project forwards or backwards at any speed

Play back manually, forwards or backwards

Figure 3.21
The Scrub Dial

In the centre of the dial you'll find two nudge buttons for moving the project cursor left or right. This is useful for working with film or video – each time you click on the nudge button it moves by one frame. The default frame rate is 24 fps (frames per second) the traditional frame rate of 35 mm film.

Edit on the move

A source of irritation to many, turning Cycle on and off during playback wasn't possible in v.1. This issue has now been rectified in v.2 and the sequencer even continues uninterrupted playback as the cycle is edited in the Ruler or Transport panel.

The thin blue line

Version 1 doesn't have a very effective fast forward and rewind feature. Use the Position Slider (the thin blue line), on the Transport bar instead. However that's all changed with v.2. The fast forwards and backwards buttons work more efficiently. However, for super fast operation press the Shift key as well.

Marking time

Setting up a Marker track (Project > Add Track > Marker) may seem a bit of a fiddle at first but it's worthwhile in the long run and saves time when navigating a large project.

They're best managed and edited in the Marker window (opened from the Project menu). There, you can change their positions and name them as verses, choruses and so on. For quick access, select a Marker track and use the Inspector, Figure 3.22.

In version 2, 'Goto Previous/Next Marker' controls have been added to the transport section, making it easier to get about in a complicated project. Setting Locator positions has also been improved, with a larger ruler and clearer numbering.

Quick tip

If the Transport panel is in the way, hide it. Use F2 on your computer keyboard to toggle it on and off.

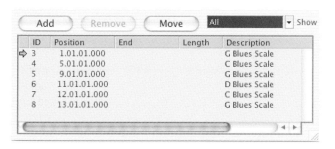

ID	Position	End	Length	Description
3	1.01.01.000			G Blues Scale
4	5.01.01.000			C Blues Scale
5	9.01.01.000			G Blues Scale
6	11.01.01.000			D Blues Scale
7	12.01.01.000			C Blues Scale
8	13.01.01.000			G Blues Scale

Add   Remove   Move   All ▼ Show

Figure 3.22
You can edit Markers in the Marker window

Figure 3.23
Add Marker and Add Cycle Marker buttons
and pop-up menus

Figure 3.23
Add Marker and Add Cycle Marker buttons
and pop-up menus

Quick tips

You can add Markers 'on the fly', at the Cursor position, during playback or in stationary mode. Use the Insert key or the Add Marker button in the Track list. Use the Add Cycle button for Cycles.

You can drag Markers – use the little red handles.

Recycling

It's tedious isn't it, having to keep setting up the locators each time you want to cycle record in a new location? Do it the easy way and store all your cycles as markers, for easy recall.

Set the left and right locators and press the Add Cycle Marker button. Store as many as you like and recall them instantly using the Cycle Marker pop-up menu.

Of course, you can add and recall ordinary markers in much the same way. Use the Add Marker button and the Locate pop-up menu, Figure 3.23.

You can also zoom in on cycle markers by using the Zoom pop-up menu.

Handy key command

Open the Marker window using Ctrl+M (on the Mac, Command+M). 0

Jumping locators

You're not sure if that bridge passage in your song works well or not. You can of course, cut it out and see how it sounds, safe in the knowledge that you can use the History list to undo things if it doesn't work. But there's a quicker way.

Set the right Locator at the beginning of the bridge section and the left Locator at the end. In other words, set them back to front. You'll notice that the Ruler turns from blue to a reddish brown colour. Start playback and the Project Cursor will skip the bridge section. This only works in v.2. If you get your locators in a twist in v.1 nothing happens at all.

Info

If Markers are set up, the Zoom menu (bottom right) will show them. Useful for zooming to Markers! – Figure 3.24.

Figure 3.24
You can zoom in on Markers

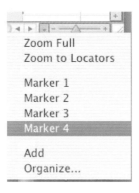

Colouring in

Colouring tracks makes them easily identifiable. So, why not colour Individual parts within a track as well? This is useful for marking out verses, choruses and bridge sections within a song as a visual alternative to the Marker track. Use the Color pop-up menu. The preset colours in version 1 are very tasteful, but far less so in version 2. You can customise the colours by choosing Select Colors… in the menu, Figure 3.25.

Importing MIDI files

If you've bought or downloaded a MIDI file from the Internet use the Import command in the File menu to open it. If it's a Type 0 MIDI file ensure the MIDI channel is set to 'Any' for correct playback. This is because Type 0 MIDI files have only one track containing up to 16 different MIDI channels. Setting the track to a specific MIDI channel would result in everything being played back with the same sound – not what you want at all. To unravel the channels on individual tracks use MIDI > Dissolve Part.

Working with MIDI took a step backwards when v.1 appeared and preparing data for export became awkward using the Merge MIDI in Loop feature. This shortcoming has been addressed with a vengeance in v.2. You can now export projects as MIDI files, without freezing the parameters and so on. The Inspector settings such as Patch, Volume and Pan are automatically inserted into the file. If you like, MIDI plug-in settings can be saved in the files as well. Similar options are available when you import MIDI files – the first Patch, Volume and Pan settings are detected and displayed in the track Inspector.

What, no project?

A common scenario: You've selected a track in project one, copied it ready to paste into project two and on switching windows project two refuses to come to life. No Inspector, no Project Cursor movement. Nothing. What's happening? Well the project isn't active. In the Project window, press the first button on the Toolbar, the 'Active project indicator'. It'll glow red (blue in v.2) and everything will spring to life, Figure 3.26a.

Renaming parts

You used to be able to name parts in Cubase 5 by selecting them and using Alt+click. That doesn't work in SX/SL but you can rename parts in the Info line. Select a part, open the Info line and type a name under 'File', Figure 3.26b.

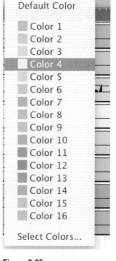

Figure 3.25
You can colour parts and tracks using the Colour pop-up menu

MIDI file tips

There are two types of MIDI file – Type 1 files which have separate tracks for each channel and Type 0 files which have just one track containing all the channels.

To import a MIDI file just drag it from the desktop (or where ever) and drop it into Cubase (v.2 only).

Figure 3.26 a
Press the button on the toolbar

Figure 3.26 b
Use the Info Line to rename parts

Info

If you move parts from one track to another, you can have them renamed, automatically by going to Preferences > Editing and ticking the Parts Get Track Names box.

Quick tip

With the Arrow tool selected, press Alt (on the Mac, Option) to split parts and events.

Figure 3.27
The Dive Track List button

Renaming events

You can rename all events on a track with the track name itself. Double click on the track name and type a new one. Press any modifier key such as Ctrl (on the Mac, Command) and press Enter. Upon closing, all the events are named.

Split screen

You can split a Track list into two sections, an upper and a lower, each with its own zoom and scroll controls (SX 2 only). Just press the Divide Track List button, Figure 3.27. This is very useful when running a video track and multiple audio tracks together because you can scroll specific audio tracks to line up directly beneath the video track, for easy reference. It's also a handy place to store Marker and Ruler tracks.

Making tracks

In version 1, audio tracks can be switched from stereo to mono and vice versa, at anytime time you like using a button on the Track List. Also, if you import an audio file v.1 will set the track to stereo or mono automatically.

This changed with the advent of v.2. Once you begin recording, you'll soon notice the absence of a Stereo/Mono switch in the Track settings, an obvious result of the new bus system. As usual, tracks are created using the Add Tracks menu. But now, when you elect to add an audio track, you're presented with a choice of mono, stereo, or a surround configuration (SX only). That's fine, but if you change your mind, or happen to be working from a template containing just mono audio tracks, changing one to stereo is no longer possible. You have to create a new track – but that's progress.

Mixer tips

Less is more

The Mixer only contains tracks that are set up in the Project window. Very sensible, because that way you only have used tracks, or those you are going to use appearing in the Mixer. This avoids the pointless giant mixer syndrome. Set up your projects, track by track instead of using templates, to keep the Mixer to a manageable size, and more importantly, increase your screen space. If you do load a template and it contains more tracks than you are likely to need – delete some, Figure 4.1.

Figure 4.1
Add tracks 'one by one' for a manageable Mixer

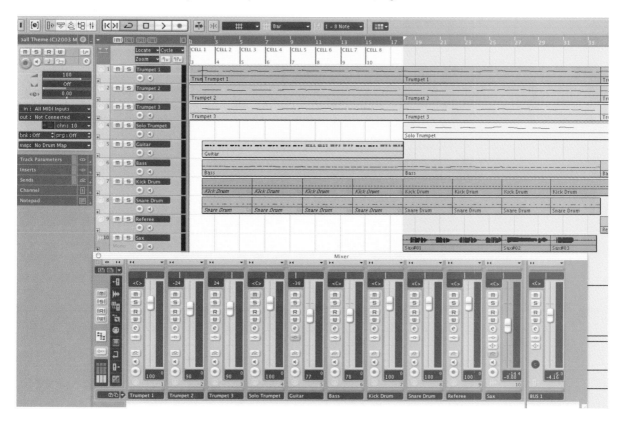

Figure 4.2
Press button 'e' to open the Channel Settings window

Why so many Mixers?

You have a choice of three Mixers in version 2 (two in SL and version 1). They're not really separate mixers, just separate views of the same one. Each one can be configured to show different combinations of channels, channel types, inserts and so on. For example – you could configure a 'MIDI only' mixer if you wanted to, and perhaps another for just audio channels. Although the configurations for each mixer are different, any changes you make in one mixer will be simultaneously mirrored in the other.

Missing extension

Cubase SL users don't have an extended Mixer. It doesn't matter too much, the extended mixer takes up space anyway. Click the button marked 'e' in the Channel strip and the VST Channel window appears, Figure 4.2. It's all there – inserts, sends and EQ. You can't have knobs on your Send Effects however. You'll have to make do with sliders. The only real disadvantage is not being able to see everything at once, but I'm sure you can live with that.

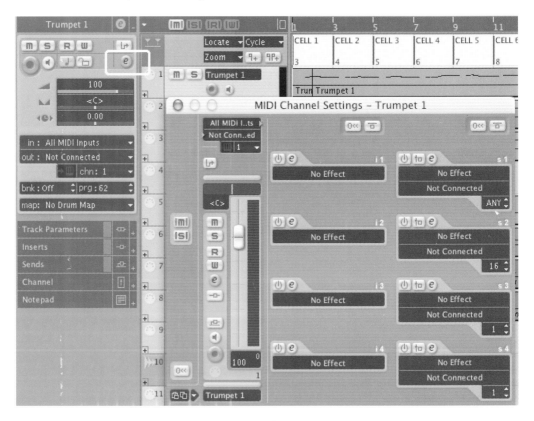

Quick mix

You don't actually have to have the Mixer open when recording or editing a single track. Use the Inspector instead. Inserts, equalisers, sends and a channel strip are all available here, plus fast access to the VST Channel window, Figure 4.3. Your settings are reflected in the Mixer.

Changing channels

When you change channels, in the Channel Settings window, it isn't necessary to close down one window and open another. A quicker way: Use the Channel Select pop-up menu, Figure 4.4. A new window opens and the old one closes.

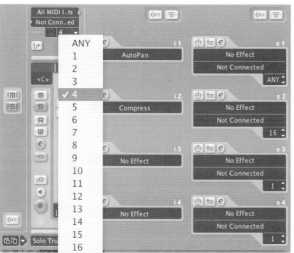

Figure 4.4
Channel Select pop-up

Figure 4.3
Mixer Channel Strip in the Inspector

Save that mix

You can save complete mixes or individual channels (audio only) as Mixer setting files. They have the extension '.vmx' and you can recall them at a later time or reload them into new projects. Right click (on the Mac, Control click) anywhere in the Mixer to bring up the Mixer context menu, Figure 4.5.

Figure 4.5
You can save your Mixer settings as .VMX files.

D' You Wanna be in My Gang

You can 'gang' as many channels as you like with 'Link Channels', found in the Mixer context menu. This is particularly useful for linking faders when mixing. For example, three brass tracks could be ganged this way. Watch out though; make new channel settings (i.e. EQ) on a linked track and they will be applied to the others as well.

> **Quick tip**
>
> Hold down the Alt key (on the Mac, Option) to alter settings separately for linked channels.

Copy and paste settings

Use the Copy and Paste buttons in the Common panel to transfer settings from one channel to another. Just select a channel, click the Copy button, select the destination channel and click the Paste button, Figures 4.6.

Hiding channels

There may be times when you don't want a certain channel or channels appearing in the Mixer. It's not immediately obvious how it works and the procedure's a bit convoluted but here's how you hide them in version 1.

• Open the View Options pop-up menu for the channel(s) and check 'Hideable', Figure 4.7.
• Open the Global View Options pop-up menu in the Common panel and uncheck the 'Hideable' option, Figure 4.8. The channel(s) will be hidden instantly.
• To restore the channels, check the 'Hideable' option in the Common panel again – Phew!

Figure 4.6
You can copy settings between channels using the Copy and Paste buttons

> **Quick tip**
>
> Hold down the Shift key for extra fader control.

Figure 4.7
Check 'Hideable' in the Channel Strip...

Figure 4.8
Uncheck 'Hideable' in the Common panel

Figure 4.9
'Can Hide' in the Common panel (SX/SL 2)

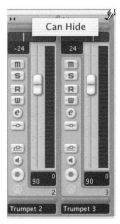

The procedure has been simplified in version 2 (thank goodness). All you have to do is select 'Can Hide' in the pop-up at the top of a Channel strip and click on the Hide Channels set to 'Can Hide' in the Common panel, Figure 4.9.

Your own views

Once you have a mixer configuration for a Project all set up you can save it as a Channel View Set. Click the Create/Select Channel View Sets buttons and select 'Add' from the pop-up menu ('Store/Remove View Set' in v.2), Figure 4.10. Type a name for the preset in the dialogue box, Figure 4.11.

Figure 4.10
You can save your Mixer configurations

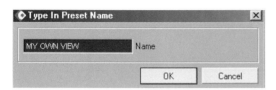

Figure 4.11
You can name your own Channel View Sets

Start from scratch

You can reset everything on a channel, including EQ, Insert and Send effects. Open the Channel Settings window and click on the Initialise Channel button, Figure 4.12. If you have version 2, you'll see the same button in the Mixer. Press it and you'll be asked if you want to reset all the channels or just the selected one.

Figure 4.12
The Initialise Channel button — click to reset channels

Quick tip

Click directly on any knob, fader or slider, whilst holding Ctrl (on the Mac, Command) to return their values to zero.

Reading and writing

You can record and play back all your Mixer actions as automation data when you activate the Read (R) and Write (W) buttons, before you start playback. A Master Automation track is created in the Project window and the data can be edited from there.

Info

The record button on the Transport panel is not used for recording automation data. Activate the Write button (W) and start playback.

Group channels

Just like hardware recording consoles, the Mixer has Group channels for controlling and treating a defined set of channels. You can add Groups to the Mixer using the Project > Add track menu. A corresponding Group track is created in the Project window.

The most obvious use for Group channels is for controlling a sub-mix. such as a drum kit. For example, you have recorded kick, snare, high-hat, high toms, low toms and overhead ambience mics on separate tracks. After setting up a volume balance for the individual tracks it makes sense to combine them in a group. This will enable you to mix the entire kit on one channel, Figure 4.13.

Quick tip

Rename your Group Channels, in the Project window or Browser, for easy identification.

Figure 4.13
Five drum tracks on a stereo Group track (SX 1)

Info

In version 1, Group tracks are always stereo. In version 2 they are configurable.

Tweak tweak

If you own a GM/GS or XG sound module of some kind you can control it in real time from within the Mixer: Open the MIDI Channel Settings window. Click in the Insert section and load the Track Control plug-in from the pop-up menu, Figure 4.14. Now you can address your sound module's parameters and effects here and tweak the controls to your hearts content.

There's another 'generic' control panel that you can select from the MIDI Insert pop-up called MIDI Control, Figure 4.15. By selecting the correct MIDI controller types, you can use this plug-in as a control panel for adjusting the sound of any MIDI instrument that receives them.

Figure 4.14 (left)
You can use Track Control to address your GM/GS/XG sound modules

Figure 4.15 (right)
MIDI Control gives you access to eight different controllers

Handy Mixer key commands

Hold Ctrl (on the Mac, Command) and click on the slider to centralise pan.
Hold Shift to increment and decrement the pan slider in single units.

A frequently asked question

Why doesn't the MIDI Channel strip have EQ facilities like the audio channel strip?

Answer: EQ is, after all, just a sophisticated tone control, applied to audio signals. MIDI channels only send and receive MIDI data; not real sound. It follows then, that you cannot apply EQ to this raw MIDI data. This is what actually happens. The MIDI data is sent to a sound module of some kind which (a) interprets the data and then (b) outputs an audio signal. That audio signal (b) has to be recorded to an audio track before EQ can be applied.

No VST Send Effects?

You may be wondering why you're unable to use the VST Send Effects, even when they are set up and active. Only the MIDI effects are available. You thought VST Instruments were routed to the audio outputs, so what's happening?

It's because VST Instruments use MIDI tracks when recording. Activate the 'Show/Hide VST Instrument Channels' button (keyboard icon) to reveal the VST Instrument channel (further to the right). The Channel Inserts and Send Effects will now be available.

In Figure 4.16 you can see that the bass, on MIDI track 2, is routed to VST Instrument track 9 (A1). Likewise, MIDI tracks 5 and 6 are routed to VST Instrument tracks 10 and 11 (also A1), where they are both treated with the FX sends.

Figure 4.16
MIDI tracks 2, 5 and 6 are routed to VST Instrument tracks 9, 10 and 11

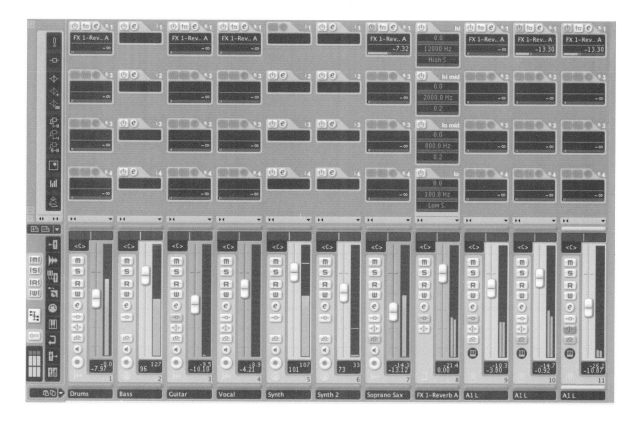

Info

You can't record on a group channel because it's never connected to an input. That's why there are no Record Enable or Monitoring buttons on group channels.

Simultaneous Reading and Writing

When recording automation data, you can watch and listen to already recorded data whilst recording further actions on another channel. Activate the Read and Write buttons simultaneously.

One way route

You can route Group channels on to further Groups – route the output of a group to another group with a higher number (to the right). However, you can't route a group to another group to the left of it in the Mixer, Figure 4.17.

Figure 4.17
Group Channel 2 is routed on to Group 3

Audio recording tips

Events, clips and files

Audio recording on a computer hard disc can be a confusing business to the unini-tiated. Of course, it's easier to understand if you are moving across from dedicat-ed hardware recording, either digital or analogue. Before you record any audio it's important to understand exactly how Cubase SX/SL handles the process. Basically, three things happen:

1 An 'audio file' is created on the computer's hard disk.
2 An 'audio clip' is also created in the Pool. This 'audio clip' is a direct reference to the 'audio file' itself which is created in your Project folder.
3 An 'audio event' is created on an audio track, in the Project window. This 'audio event' plays back the 'audio clip'.

In other words, Events play the Clip which communicates with the Audio File.

As if that isn't complicated enough, specific audio regions can be created from clips and events – phew!

Bus routes

Getting music in and out of Cubase is more flexible than ever with version 2 because you can configure as many input and output busses as you like. Mono, stereo or surround format (SX only) are all possible. Configurations are made in the new VST Connections window and saved along with your projects, Figure 5.1. For this reason it makes sense to first set up your busses and then save them as tem-plates. If you need different busses for different projects you can also save them as presets for instant recall.

How many busses do you need? It depends on your hardware and the amount of inputs and outputs you have. If you have a basic stereo card, such as the M-Audio Audiophile, then a bus assigned to the two analogue inputs will be needed. A separate bus could be assigned to just one of those inputs, for mono recording (recording individual instruments, or a vocal). Another bus could be assigned to the digital stereo inputs. You'll also need a bus for the stereo out and digital out.

If you have a more complex set-up, with multiple ins and outs, then obviously you can set up more busses. You will also be able to use the surround sound capabilities that Cubase SX has to offer.

Figure 5.1
Busses are configured in the VST Connections window

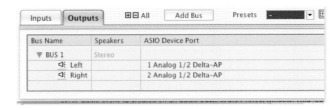

| Inputs | Outputs | ⊞⊟ All | Add Bus | Presets | ▾ |

Bus Name	Speakers	ASIO Device Port
▼ BUS 1	Stereo	
◁ Left		1 Analog 1/2 Delta–AP
◁ Right		2 Analog 1/2 Delta–AP

Naming is the game

Before you set up a surround sound bus, name the inputs and outputs on your audio hardware – Left, Right, Centre and so on. Now, if you're working with a colleague, you can both have the same names for the set-up, regardless of different hardware. It's a time-saver because Cubase will automatically locate the correct inputs and outputs when your projects are loaded on either computer.

It's also a good idea to name your input and output busses. Something simple like Stereo in, Mono in and Digital Out will do. Of course, you can give them silly names if you prefer.

Which sample rate?

Quick tip

Once you have decided on a sample rate, stick with it throughout the project.

Basically, the higher the rate the better the sound quality. What's actually available depends on your audio hardware. For example, if you have a popular sound card from the M-Audio Delta range you'll have a choice of anything between 8 kHz and 96 kHz. Most people work with 44.1 kHz which is the happy medium. If your project is destined for a CD, that's how it will end up anyway. By all means use 96 kHz, if you have the capability, but remember it will use more disk space and processing power. There's little point though in going lower than 44.1 kHz because audio quality will deteriorate noticeably from 32 kHz down. Setting a sample rate is done in the Project Setup, Figure 5.2.

Which record format?

Quick tip

Although the sample rate must remain fixed for a project you can change the bit depth (sample resolution) at any time.

Cubase SX/SL supports 16 bit, 24 bit and 32 bit recording. If your audio hardware only supports 16 bit there's nothing to be gained by selecting 24 bit except larger files with the same audio quality. However, if your hardware supports it, choose a higher resolution. Bear in mind though that higher resolutions result in larger audio files, thereby putting more strain on your computer. Setting the record format is done in the Project Setup, Figure 5.3.

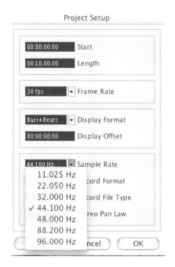
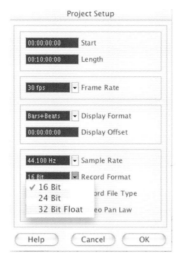

Figures 5.2 and 5.3
Sample rate and record format are both set
up in the Projct Setup window

Which file type?

You have a choice of three file types when you record – AIFF Files, Wave Files and Broadcast Wave Files. Which type you choose depends largely on whether you use a PC or Mac computer. Choosing a file type is done in the Project Setup, Figure 5.4. Generally speaking choose 'AIFF File' if you're working on a Mac (although you can record Wave files) and 'Wave File' if you're working on a PC.

If you wish to embed details such as Author, Description and Reference text into a file choose 'Broadcast Wave File', Figure 5.5. This is useful if you intend transferring the files to another computer. Adding the text is done in the Preferences section. In fact you can export any file type as a Broadcast Wave File when you export an audio file (File > Export . Audio Mixdown…). On choosing the 'Broadcast Wave File' as a file type you are given the option to add the text before completing the process, Figure 5.6. You can also specify a time code position here as well, for use in video projects and so on. This is set, by default, to the start position of the exported audio in the project (the left locator position), but you can alter this to whatever you want.

A fourth file type is available in version 2 – Wave 64 (SX only). This format is a good choice for live recordings because they can be much larger than ordinary WAV files.

Figure 5.4
You set the file type in the Project window

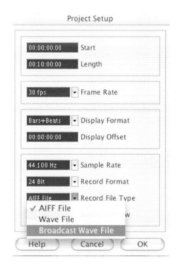

Figure 5.5
You can embed copyright details in
Broadcast Wave Files

New bus routes

As a result of the new VST 2.3 audio engine in version 2, signal routing and record-ing audio is slightly different to before. The busses you first set up in the VST Connections window appear in the Mixer as input and output channels (SX only). They look much the same as regular audio channels but have their own dividers and horizontal scroll bars.

The Input channel is placed to the left of the audio channels and the Output channel to their right. Visually they're identical twins, except that the Input chan-nel doesn't have a Solo button.

When recording, you check the signal levels using the Input channel – in 'Input VU' mode, Figure 5.7.

Figure 5.7
Checking the Input level

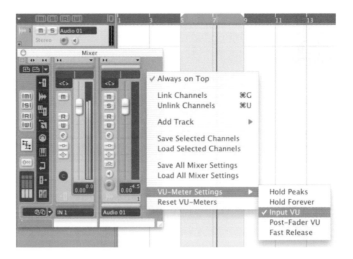

When that's done you switch to 'Post-Fader VU' mode and check the output level – the signal being recorded on your hard disk, Figure 5.8. Only the output bus is visible in SL and the input levels are checked using the channel strip on the audio track itself, the same as in SX/SL 1.

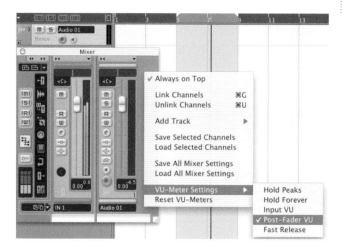

Figure 5.8
Checking the output level of the input bus
(the level to be recorded)

The recorded audio is viewed and controlled on a normal channel strip, Figure 5.9.

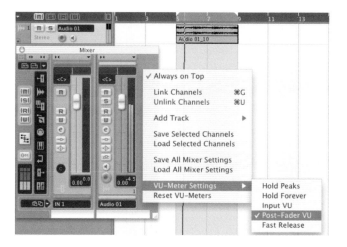

Figure 5.9
Playing back the recorded audio

Avoid the red light area

If you've been using an analogue tape recorder you'll know that it's possible to occasionally drive the record levels into the red without fear of distortion. On analogue tape this amounts to a form of compression and can provide a bigger, warmer sound. However, try it on a digital recorder and you'll end up with nothing of the sort – just distortion. By all means keep as close to the red area as possible but be careful not to exceed it.

True Tape

If digital recording is too cold and clinical sounding for you, ignore the advice about going into the red (immediately above) and try using True Tape as an Insert effect. (v.1), Figure 5.10. This feature (available only in SX, not SL) simulates analogue tape saturation. In other words, you can drive the meters into the red without fear of distortion.

However care is still needed. Raising the Drive Control, on the True Tape panel, raises the level of the audio file and it may well reach clipping level. That's nothing to worry about in SX itself because True Tape converts all signals to 32 bit float format (which is virtually distortion free). But it's worth turning True Tape off, just to check that clipping is not occurring in the audio hardware.

Figure 5.10
Use True Tape to recreate the sound of analogue tape saturation

Figure 5.11
Use Magneto (Dynamic plug-in) for realistic 'tape saturation'.

Warm up

A new plug-in, Magneto, replaces True Tape in version 2 adding the positive qualities of analogue recording – warmth, punch, brilliance and so on – after it's been digitally recorded. The algorithm behind it is based on Steinberg's studies and measurements of analogue tape recorders, the results of which were then transferred to SX, Figure 5.11.

'Drive' is the main parameter and it's used to set the simulated analogue tape recording level while the audio is played back. The changes take effect more or less immediately and doing it like this helps you to experiment and get a feeling for how the settings interact.

Three 'Level' buttons are used to switch between three different Meter modes: Input – the level of the input signal is shown: onTape – the meters show an equivalent of the level recorded on the simulated 'tape' and Output which shows the output level for the entire plug-in.

Wet or dry?

For obvious reasons we usually record audio signals 'dry', without effects and EQ, (that double delayed digeridoo might not sound quite so good on mix-down).

However, should you want to, version 2 has facilities that allow you to treat the incoming audio with EQ and Insert effects (SX only). If you do record this way Steinberg recommend that you take advantage of their 32 Bit Float record format, to avoid digital distortion. The reason for this is that the effect processing in the input channel is done in 32 Bit Float format anyway. If you record at 16 or 24 Bit, the audio will be converted to this lower resolution when it's written to file and might result in a poorer signal.

Your own input

Many users mistakenly assume that when recording, you set the input levels using the channel strip fader. Of course, if you think about it this can't be so. The fader only affects the playback of the audio once it's recorded. So when recording, remember, the level meters show the signal level at the 'input' selected for the audio channel. You can adjust this level in one of the following ways:

- By adjusting the output level of the sound source (synthesiser, or whatever) or your external mixer.
- By using your audio hardware's own software mixer to set the input levels, if this is provided, Figure 5.12.

Figure 5.12
Some audio cards, like the Audiophile, have a software mixer

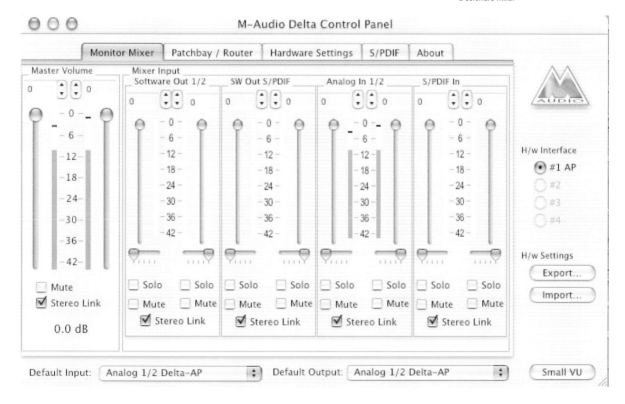

Record enable

You've probably noticed that enabling tracks for recording is automatic (by default) whenever you select a track. You can switch this off in the Preferences > Edit page by un-checking Enable Record on Selected Tracks. Having it on all the time can be irritating, particularly if you are used to using a conventional hardware recorder.

Multitrack confusion

A frequently asked question – I thought that Cubase SX/SL recorded several tracks of audio at a time, like a conventional tape recorder. I can't get this to work. How's it done?

You can record on as many audio tracks as your computer's processing power can handle. The main limitation to this is your audio hardware. If you have a stereo sound card, then only two inputs will show up in the VST Connections window (in version 1, the VST Inputs window), Figure 5.13 and 5.14. In this case you can only record two sound sources at once (although a single source may contain a mix of different instruments) and further overdubbing will probably be required.

If you have a multi-input card, any amount of inputs (depending on the card) will show up in the VST Inputs window. They can, of course, be routed to different audio channels.

Figure 5.13
The VST Inputs window, SX 1

Figure 5.14
The VST Connections window, SX 2

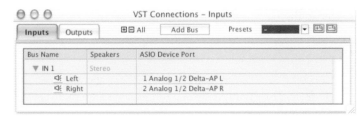

Recording vocals

To record vocals properly you'll need a directional mic. If you can afford it, a condenser mic is best. Companies like AKG produce a range to suit most pockets but there are also quite a few cheap, but decent, Chinese condenser models around. Failing that a quality dynamic mic such as the trusty Shure SM57 or SM58 will still produce good results.

Although most vocal mics have built-in wind shields it's still a good idea to use a pop screen. Apart from preventing sudden pops, if you are recording a vocalist other than yourself, it will also prevent them getting too close to the microphone.

A distance of between 15 and 60 cm between the mouth and mic is usual with the mic tilted slightly, either up or down, away from a direct line with the mouth.

A greater distance is fine but bear in mind the fact that more gain may be needed if the vocalist has a quiet voice. Problems with background noise could arise. Keep the mic away from reflective surfaces, walls being an obvious example.

Recording electric guitars

Small practice amps are ideal for recording guitars but the sound is reflected off the floor and colours the tone. The answer – place the amp on a chair, half a metre or so above the ground.

A dynamic mic such as the Shure SM58 is the usual choice for the job. To begin with place it between 15 and 30 cm from the centre of one of the speakers in the amp cabinet. Experiment by moving it off centre from there, to alter the tone. Try using two mics, one further away or at the side, or even behind the speaker cabinet. Use a similar method for bass guitar, but place it further away to avoid a boxy sound. Alternatively, record the Bass direct.

Recording acoustic guitars

Nylon string guitars are not loud instruments. You'll need a sensitive microphone to record them properly, preferably a condenser with a flat frequency response as opposed to a vocal mic.

Aim the mic somewhere between the sound hole and the end of the neck, but keep your distance, maybe as far as 45 cm.

If you're a singer songwriter you probably prefer to record guitar and vocal together. Tilt the vocal mic upwards a little and the guitar mic down, to avoid phase cancelled signals.

To capture the richness of good acoustic guitar, try seating the player in a room with a reflective floor – wood or stone as opposed to carpet. Alternatively, place a large piece of wood under the chair.

Recording brass

Brass instruments produce high sound pressure levels (SPL) so choose your mic carefully. Condensers with a large diaphragm and flat response are best. Remember to use the pre attenuation switch to cope with the high SPL.

Place the mic slightly off axis when mic'ing trumpets and trombones because although the higher frequencies are projected in front of the bell, the lower ones are spread over a wider area.

Recording strings

Recording a violin can be tricky. For a start, violinists tend to move about a lot. Ask the player to sit down. This also helps reflections from the ceiling. Use a flat response cardoid mic like the Shure Performance PG 81 placed over the bridge. The distance depends on the style of music and the type of sound you want. Basically, the closer you go, the scratchier it gets.

Small string ensembles are quite easy to record. Use a crossed pair of mics (at right angles to each other) above the players.

You can also tape two boundary mics, one either side of a 1 metre square piece of plywood and suspend that above and in front of the musicians. This should produce a great stereo image.

Recording acoustic bass

A combination of pickup and mic usually works okay. Experiment with the mic placement, starting fairly close to the bridge.

Recording grand piano

Most musicians have neither the space nor the money for a grand piano in their home studio. If you're one of the lucky few, place a condenser microphone about 30 cm above the bass strings and another the same distance above the treble strings. AKG C 535 mics are a good choice here.

Another way – tape a couple of boundary mics to the underside of the lid and close it.

Recording upright piano

The average musician is more likely to have a beer stained upright in the corner of his studio than a full size grand. If that's you, open the lid and place two directional condensers, one at each end, above the treble and bass strings.

If that doesn't work, take off the front panel and place the mics in front of the strings.

Another way – use two boundary mics, taped to the wall, behind the piano. You can only do this if it's an overdub because boundary mics pick up other instruments in the room. Alternatively tape them to the front panel, inside, near the hammers.

Recording bagpipes

Well, you never know? Mic the chanter (finger holes) and the drone pipes separately.

Monitor your input

Once you've laid down an initial track (or group of tracks) you'll need to hear the music back as you record any further overdubs. The process is known as 'monitoring' and there are three ways to do it in Cubase. Which one you choose depends on your hardware and your preferred method of working.

If hearing things back with the panning in place along with effects and EQ is important to you then monitoring via Cubase itself is the way to go. Using this method, the input signal is mixed with the audio playback. This is ideal if you like a touch of reverb on your voice or you need to hear a certain effect on your guitar while you are recording. However there is a drawback – latency. The signal you hear back will be slightly delayed. It might not be much but even a delay of 20 milliseconds or so can be very off-putting to most musicians. The latency value depends on your audio hardware and drivers and it's usually possible to lower them by reducing the size and number of buffers in the VST Multitrack panel (Devices > Device Setup…).

If your audio hardware is ASIO 2 compatible you may be able to use Direct Monitoring. The audio hardware handles the monitoring and sends the input signal directly out again. You can easily check to see if you have this facility by opening the VST Multitrack Setup panel. If the Direct Monitoring check box is greyed out you don't have it. If it isn't, you're up and running with Direct Monitoring. However you can't use any EQ or effects because the signal doesn't actually pass through SX/SL. Cubase just 'controls' the monitoring.

The most straightforward way to monitor your performance is to use an external mixer. It needn't be expensive. Something small, like a Spirit Notepad is ideal. This way a signal is sent to your main studio monitor speakers and an additional feed is sent from the mixer's auxiliary sends to your sound card. If the mixer has direct outputs use those instead.

Quick tip

If you're using an external mixer for monitoring ensure that 'Manual' mode is selected in Preferences > VST Auto Monitoring and leave the Monitor buttons off when recording.

Well stacked

One of the best things about recording with a sequencer is the ability to cycle record, and it's now become easier than ever in version 2. A brilliant new cycle record mode allows you to stack multiple takes on a single audio track. With 'Stacked' selected and 'Punch In' and 'Cycle' activated on the Transport panel, cycle recording takes place as normal. But – and this is the best bit – when you've finished recording, all the takes are stacked on the one audio track, each with a different number. By chopping them up into smaller events and choosing the best of the bunch you can quickly assemble a perfect take (well that's the theory anyway), Figure 5.15.

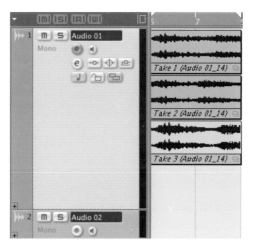

Figure 5.15
Three 'takes' stacked on a single track

Info

You can only play back one audio event at a time on a single audio track. If you happen to record over part of a previously recorded event and create an overlap, only the visible event will be played back.

Quick tip

Use 'Move to Front' and 'Move to Back' (Edit menu) to get at overlapping events.

Check the trash

Everybody finds their own way of doing things when recording in Cubase. Cycle recording (mentioned above) being just one method. You can also do it the old fashioned way, by recording a 'take', listening back and if you like it, great, you keep it. If you don't, you can delete it and record another one. But here's the clever bit. In Cubase this 'take' – referred to as an audio event – is not actually deleted, but remains on the hard disk, in the Pool's Trash folder, so you can change your mind and recall it later. Just don't empty the trash!

Punch in/out

Playing an instrument and recording your performance at the same time can be an unwieldy, and potentially dangerous task to say the least (pressing record buttons on and off and so on). Fortunately the whole process can be automated in Cubase.

For example – you need to drop in and repair a guitar solo between bars 17 and 21. Set the Locators to encompass those bars and activate the Punch In and Punch Out buttons on the Transport panel. Now scroll back to a point before the drop in – let's say bar 13 – and activate playback. When the cursor reaches bar 17 the sequencer begins recording and when it reaches bar 21 it stops (playback continues), Figure 5.16.

Figure 5.16
Punch in and Out recording in SX 1

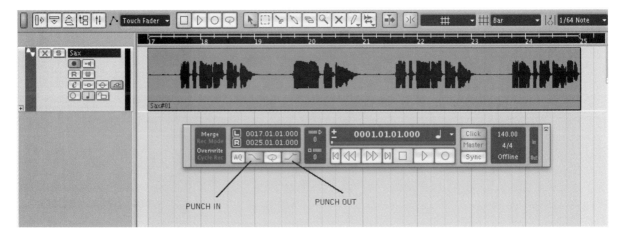

No more delay

You may have experienced some degree of plug-in delay in previous versions Cubase – that brief moment of time it takes for a plug-in to process the audio being fed into it. The result is a slightly delayed output signal. Good news – it's now a thing of the past in version 2 because full plug-in delay compensation throughout the audio path is now provided. It's switched on by default but should you, for some reason need to turn it off it, you can do so in the Plug-In Information window.

Making waves

Creating waveform images as you actually record is all very well but it's CPU inten-sive. If you find things are slowing down as a result, turn it off – go to Preferences > Audio (v.1) or Preferences > Record (v.2) and un-tick the 'Create Images dur-ing Record' box.

MIDI recording tips

Start right

In common with other MIDI sequencers, Cubase sometimes plays back the wrong sounds from time to time. To prevent this happening, create a one bar set-up part and manually insert a program number for each track. This is best done using the List Editor, Figure 6.1.

Figure 6.1
Set-up bar with Program, Expression, Chorus (ExtEff 3) and Reverb (ExtEff 1)

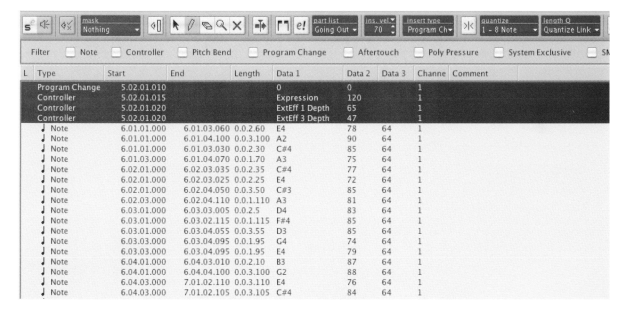

L	Type	Start	End	Length	Data 1	Data 2	Data 3	Channe	Comment
	Program Change	5.02.01.010			0	0		1	
	Controller	5.02.01.015			Expression	120		1	
	Controller	5.02.01.020			ExtEff 1 Depth	65		1	
	Controller	5.02.01.020			ExtEff 3 Depth	47		1	
♪	Note	6.01.01.000	6.01.03.060	0.0.2.60	E4	78	64	1	
♪	Note	6.01.01.000	6.01.04.100	0.0.3.100	A2	90	64	1	
♪	Note	6.01.01.000	6.01.03.030	0.0.2.30	C#4	85	64	1	
♪	Note	6.01.03.000	6.01.04.070	0.0.1.70	A3	75	64	1	
♪	Note	6.02.01.000	6.02.03.035	0.0.2.35	C#4	77	64	1	
♪	Note	6.02.01.000	6.02.03.025	0.0.2.25	E4	72	64	1	
♪	Note	6.02.01.000	6.02.04.050	0.0.3.50	C#3	85	64	1	
♪	Note	6.02.03.000	6.02.04.110	0.0.1.110	A3	81	64	1	
♪	Note	6.03.01.000	6.03.03.005	0.0.2.5	D4	83	64	1	
♪	Note	6.03.01.000	6.03.02.115	0.0.1.115	F#4	85	64	1	
♪	Note	6.03.01.000	6.03.04.055	0.0.3.55	D3	85	64	1	
♪	Note	6.03.03.000	6.03.04.095	0.0.1.95	G4	74	64	1	
♪	Note	6.03.03.000	6.03.04.095	0.0.1.95	E4	79	64	1	
♪	Note	6.04.01.000	6.04.03.010	0.0.2.10	B3	87	64	1	
♪	Note	6.04.01.000	6.04.04.100	0.0.3.100	G2	88	64	1	
♪	Note	6.04.03.000	7.01.02.110	0.0.3.110	E4	76	64	1	
♪	Note	6.04.03.000	7.01.02.105	0.0.3.105	C#4	84	64	1	

Chase up

If you start playback from a point other than the beginning of a project, you may hear the wrong sounds. Use the Chase Events Filter in the Preference settings to ensure that Cubase chases the MIDI events. Check only the event types that you don't want chased, Figure 6.2.

Figure 6.2
The MIDI-Chase Events Filter

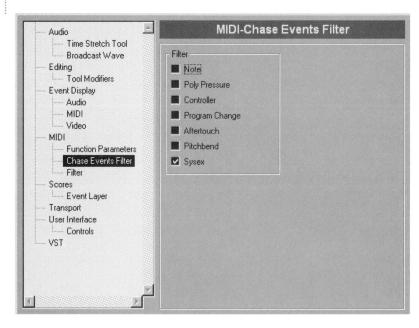

Cycle tracks

One of the most useful things about recording MIDI in Cubase is the option to record in a cycle or loop. You can set up a loop by positioning the left and right locator and activating the Cycle button on the Transport panel.

Dangerous doubles

Watch out when cycle recording and quantize are combined; there's a danger of double notes being recorded. These not only sound strange but can cause problems such as stuck notes on some synthesisers.

They're easily spotted in the Score Editor where they show up as note clusters. Fortunately, you can erase them quickly using MIDI > Functions > Delete Doubles, Figure 6.3.

Figure 6.3
Deleting doubled notes

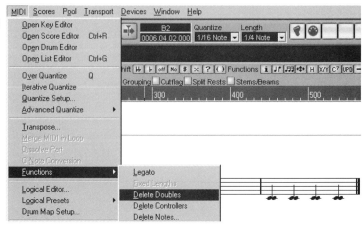

Figure 6.4
Set an appropriate record mode on the Transport panel

A pile up

Stacked recording is available when you cycle record in version 2, and jolly useful it is too. On each pass a new part is created and given it's own 'lane' in the track. When you've finished recording, you can choose the best bits from each 'take' and join them together using the Merge MIDI in Loop feature.

What's the catch?

If you're prone to playing a little ahead of the beat when recording, you've probably experienced the annoying habit Cubase has of not recording your first note. To prevent this from happening raise the Record Catch Range in the MIDI Preferences.

Retro record

We lost it in SX1, but it's back in SX 2 – the option to record everything into the buffer memory. Check the Retrospective Record option in the Preferences (Record page). Now, if a MIDI track is record enabled and you happen to be doodling about in stop mode or even during playback, everything you play is recorded in the buffer. To hear it, check 'Retrospective Recording' (Transport menu) and a MIDI part will magically appear, Figures 6.5 and 6.6.

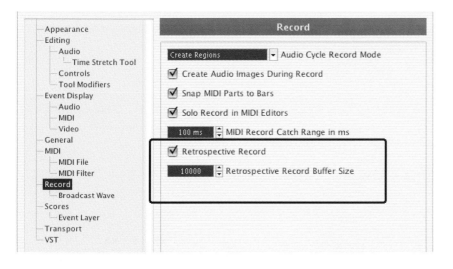

Figure 6.5
Preferences - Retrospective Recording

Figure 6.6
Transport menu - Retrospective Record

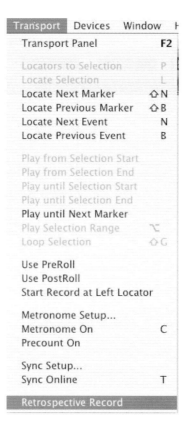

The hidden sound module

If you need a General MIDI sound source for your music why not use the Universal Sound Module? Figure 6.7. What's that? Well, it's a very useful, 16 channel, multi-timbral virtual software synth. Where is it? Ah! now that's a well kept secret. It was first included with Cubase 5 and it's also included with SX/SL. You'll find it in the Cubase 5 Instruments folder. For some reason though, Steinberg seem reluctant to tell anybody about it. It's a VST Instrument and is loaded in the normal way. It features four stereo outputs which are particularly useful for routing sounds to inserts and sends in the Mixer.

Figure 6.7
The Universal Sound Module

Get real

If your music uses acoustic samples and you're after a realistic interpretation of real instruments, forget the keyboard and concentrate on the virtual instrument you are recording. For example, if it's a violin, imagine yourself actually playing it. Become that violinist. The same applies to any instrument. Try to get inside the mind of your virtual musician. Before you can do this confidently, you will almost certainly need to spend time listening to real instruments in the hands of expert performers.

Mind the gap

When emulating monophonic instruments (those that play one note at a time such as woodwind and brass), be careful not to create overlaps when playing from the keyboard. If it happens, clean them up, from within the editor window you are using, with MIDI > Functions > Delete Overlaps mono/poly, Figure 6.8.

Figure 6.8
Deleting overlapping notes

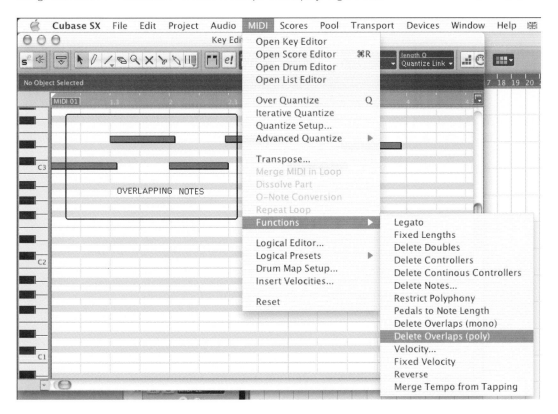

Multiple notes

Overlapping notes of the same pitch, sometimes referred to as multiple notes cause problems on some synths. Avoid them using Length Correction, found in the MIDI Preferences. You can adjust the length of notes, of the same pitch and MIDI channel, so that there always is a short time between the end of one note and the start of another. The default setting is -2 ticks.

Pitch bend and modulation

Use controllers such as pitch bend and modulation to help to make sampled sounds more convincing. It's best done whilst playing, using the pitch bend controller on the MIDI keyboard. You can add the pitch bend afterwards but it's hard to beat the spontaneity of playing it live. Vibrato is often used on strings and wind instruments and you can achieve this by adding modulation. Go easy though, to avoid that 'nanny goat' sound.

Another way to add pitch bend. In the Key Editor, click on the arrow, just below te keyboard, on the lower-left side of the screen. A menu appears. Choose 'Pitch Bend' and a graphic representation appears in the controller display. Pitch bend can be drawn and edited here using the Pencil tool. Of course you are not restricted to just pitch bend and modulation here. All the usual MIDI controllers appear on the menu, Figure 6.9.

Figure 6.9
You can draw Pitch Bend and Modulation and so on, in the Controller Lane

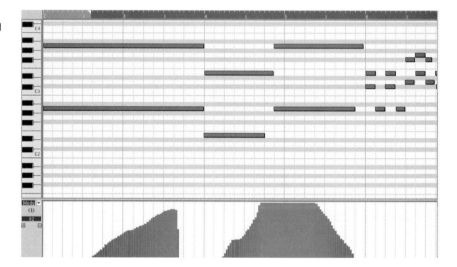

Smooth things over

To smooth things out, after playing a long flowing line (strings maybe), select the recorded notes in the Score or Key Editors and apply Legato (MIDI > Functions > Legato), Figure 6.10. Set a suitable legato overlap with Preferences > MIDI > Function Parameters > Legato Overlap (SX 2 – Editing page).

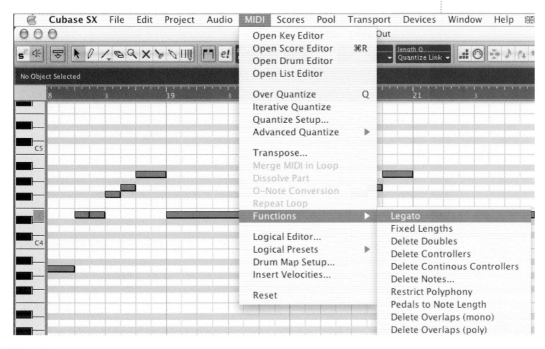

Weeding

When playing a MIDI keyboard, particularly the mini variety, it's very easy to leave unwanted 'ghost notes' scattered about the track. These are usually very short in duration and weak in velocity value. Although you can't always hear them they can wreak havoc on some sound modules. Weed them out by using MIDI > Functions > Delete Notes... Figure 6.11.

Figure 6.10
Applying Legato

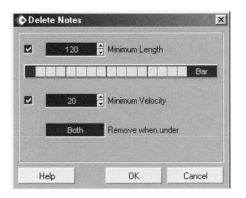

Figure 6.11
After selecting 'Delete Notes', you set the criteria using this dialogue box

Avoid dropout

Too many voices sounding at once in a busy MIDI sequence can result in unpredictable dropping out of notes if your instrument has limited polyphony. You can restrict the number of voices used with MIDI > Functions > Restrict Polyphony. Just enter a value, Figure 6.12.

Figure 6.12
Restricting Polyphony

Just velocity

There's a very handy dialogue box for increasing, reducing, compressing and limiting velocity values under MIDI > Function > Velocity..., Figure 6.13.

Use Fixed Velocity, from the same menu, to force all selected events to correspond with the Insert Velocity feature on the Key Editor toolbar. Use it on selected events in the Project window or any of the MIDI editors including the Score.

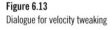

Figure 6.13
Dialogue for velocity tweaking

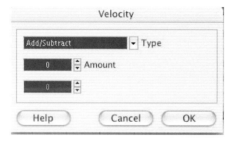

Smoother playing

If you're not too hot on the keyboard your MIDI recordings may sound a bit lumpy due to uneven playing. To avoid this, smooth the velocity data as you play using the Velocity Shift and Velocity Compress track parameters, Figure 6.14. If you want to make the data permanent use the MIDI Merge in Loop function.

Figure 6.14
Compress as you play

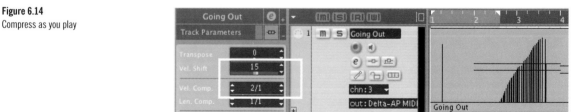

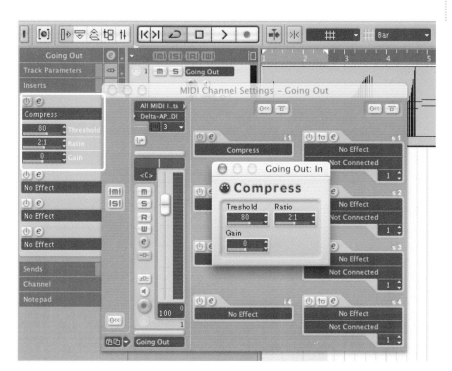

Figure 6.15
Compress – the audio style approach to MIDI compression

Human touch

Again, if you're a technically challenged keyboard player, you may well use quantize to correct your playing. If so, your recordings may sound a little mechanical. To loosen things up a bit use the Random settings in the Track parameters. Select 'Position' from the pop-up menu, play the track and vary the Min and Max parameters in real time until it sounds loose enough, Figure 6.16. You can also randomise velocity, note length and pitch from here. Random pitch! Oh well, each to his own.

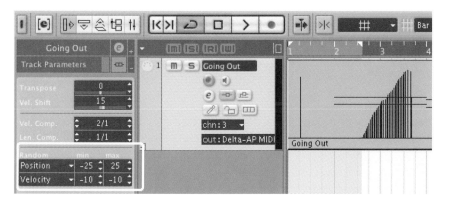

Figure 6.16
Randomising Position and Velocity parameters

Plug-in fun

The MIDI plug-ins with Cubase SX/SL are a great way of generating ideas for arrangements and compositions. Try experimenting, there's much fun to be had. If you're not quite sure how to begin, try this trick:

1 Select a MIDI track and set the output to either a GM grand piano sound or set up the A1 synth and choose a LEAD preset such as Holl-O-Kord WMF, Figure 6.17.

Figure 6.17
Set up the A1 synth

2 Open the Inserts folder and choose the Chorder MIDI plug-in, Figure 6.18. This is a MIDI chord processor. Pressing a single key on your MIDI keyboard will play complete chords depending on the settings chosen.

Figure 6.18
The Chorder plug-in

3 Set Chorder to Global mode and from the Preset menu, select a chord type. A straight major chord will serve the purpose to begin with.
4 Set the tempo to 120 bpm (default) and using single keys, record a simple four bar sequence, something like one bar of C, one bar of D and two bars of A, Figure 6.19.

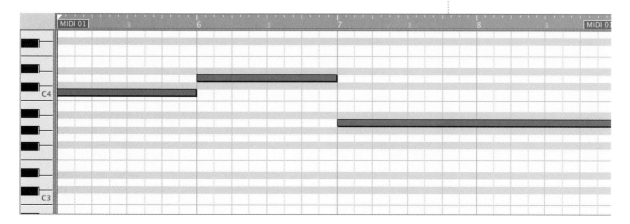

5 Set up a four bar cycle and play it back. You should now be hearing complete major chords whereever a key was pressed. Okay, that sequence on its own is not going to set the world on fire. To make it more interesting:

6 Open the Inserts folder again. There are still three more insert slots available. In the second one, choose Arpache 5, Figure 6.20. Arpache 5 is an arpeggiator. Experiment with the presets and quantize settings. The 'simple up-down' preset works well combined with a quantize value of 16T.

Figure 6.19
Draw or record a few notes

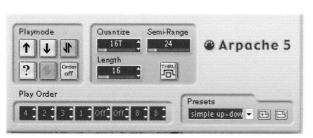

Figure 6.20
The Arpache 5 arpeggiator

7 In the third insert slot, select AutoPan, Figure 6.21. The 'left and right and…' preset provides an interesting, constantly changing stereo picture.

8 Save the result of this as a Project file and name it plugins.cpr. There's more to come…

Figure 6.21
Select Autopan

Control freak

If you use a GM/GS or XG compatible MIDI device and you'd like instant control over the presets use the Track Control MIDI plug-in, Figure 4.14 (page 42). If you used this type of instrument with the above trick, load Track Control into the fourth Insert slot and experiment. An awful lot can be done here to liven up a boring synth preset.

Step by step

If you're into step sequencers there's a perfectly adequate one in the MIDI plug-ins folder. To find out how it works and add a simple bass line to the above trick, follow these steps:

* Open the above the project that you saved earlier called plugins.cpr .
* Select a new MIDI track and channel and set the output to VB -1.
* Choose the 'Synth Bass' preset, Figure 6.22.

Figure 6.22
Choose the 'Synth Bass' preset in the VB-1

* Open the Inserts folder and choose the Step Designer MIDI plug-in. Step Designer is a MIDI pattern sequencer, that sends out MIDI notes and controller data, Figure 6.23.

Figure 6.23
Step Designer MIDI plug-in is a MIDI pattern sequencer

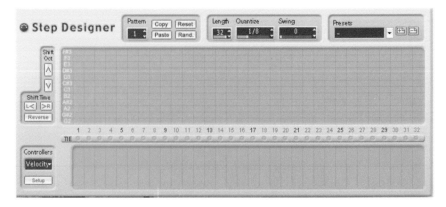

- Change the Quantize setting to 1/8 and change the Length setting to 32. This will give us four bars of eighth note steps to play with.
- Fill in all the squares on the A2 line with the mouse pointer. Use the Shift Octave arrows to drop it two octaves. Play it back. You now have a simple bass line accompanying the arpeggios.

Shut the gate

To make notes shorter in Step Designer, select 'Gate' on the Controllers pop-up menu and lower the bars in the controller display. To make notes longer, you can tie two notes together. Insert two notes and click the Tie button below the second note.

Transposing parts

A common problem: There's a four bar section on a piano track that you would like to transpose. The Transpose feature in the Track Parameters folder transposes the whole track. What do you do?

Solution: With the Scissors tool, make the four bars you need to transpose into an individual part. Now select it and use the Transpose feature (MIDI menu) to alter the pitch of the notes

Hidden data

A common problem: You've made a really great track using the Chorder and Arpache MIDI plug-ins as Inserts and you want to turn it into MIDI data but there's nothing showing up in the editors.

Solution: To turn all your MIDI plug-in data into real events on this track use the Merge MIDI in Loop feature (MIDI menu).

- In the Project window, mute any tracks you want left out of the operation.
- Set up the left and right locators around the area you want to convert.
- Select an empty track and use MIDI > Merge MIDI in Loop.
- A dialogue box appears – check the 'Include Inserts' and click OK. A new part appears on the destination track.
- Open the List Editor and you'll find a veritable mass of data!

Quick tip

You can create up to 100 different patterns in Step Designer. Build a sequence by playing them back in the order you require by drawing them in the automation sub track. If Pattern Select is not on the menu, choose More... to add it to the list.

Time and tempo tips

Take your pick

You have two choices for creating and editing tempo changes and inserting time signatures – the Tempo Track and the List Editor. So which one do you use? Well, creating and editing tempo events is easiest in the Tempo Track. Events are displayed in a graphical form; time – horizontally, and tempo – vertically. However precise editing of events is best done in the Project Browser, where both the Tempo Track and the Signature Track information is presented in a numerical list form, Figure 7.1.

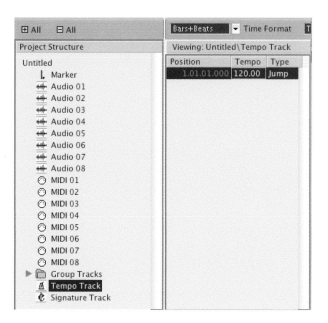

Figure 7.1
You can edit time and tempo events in the Project Browser

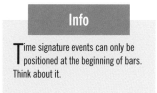

Time signature events can only be positioned at the beginning of bars. Think about it.

73

Change your signature

Here's a quick way to enter a time signature change in the Tempo Track. Hold down the Alt key (on the Mac, Option), and click with the mouse in the signature area (just below the ruler). The new entry will always be 4/4, whatever the time signature at the beginning of the project. However, you can edit it afterwards with the two thumb-wheel controls for the Signature display.

Slow down

If you can't play something at a fast tempo, slow it down. Why struggle? Computers don't make everything in life easy (the opposite is often the case), but they can certainly help the 'technically challenged' MIDI keyboard players amongst us.

For example – you're recording at 120 bpm and suddenly come up against a passage that you can't play at that speed. On the Transport panel, turn off the Tempo Track (in v.1 the Master tempo), and scroll the tempo to something more comfortable, like 80 bpm. After recording the awkward passage you can turn the Tempo Track back on, to hear the track at the right speed again.

The right click

Does the sound of the Cubase metronome drive you crazy? The default audio click generated by the metronome becomes tiresome after a while, to say the least – but it can be changed to something much easier on the ear. Change it in the Metronome Setup, opened from the Transport menu.

You can choose between an audio or MIDI click or a combination of both. The audio click is played back via your audio hardware but the MIDI click can be sent to another external device such as a drum machine or synthesiser. Many musicians like a hi-hat sound as a tempo guide and setting one up is quite simple. Here's an example using the VSTi LM-7 drum module included with Cubase. Follow these steps:

- Load and activate the LM-7 drum module, Figure 7.2. Select the Compressor drum set.
- Open the Metronome Setup and put a tick in the MIDI Click box, Figure 7.3.
- Select 'LM-7 in the MIDI device pop-up menu and enter these values in their respective boxes:
    * Channel: 1–16 (choose any channel).
    * High Note: A#1.
    * High Velocity: 100.
    * Low Note G#1.
    * Low Velocity 80.

In 4/4 time, the metronome will now play back an open hi-hat on the first beat of the bar (the High Note value – A#1)and a closed hi-hat on the second, third and fourth beats (the Low Note value – G#1). Because the higher note has a velocity of 100 it provides a strong downbeat at the beginning of each bar and the open high-hat re-enforces this.

Figure 7.2
The LM-7 drum machine

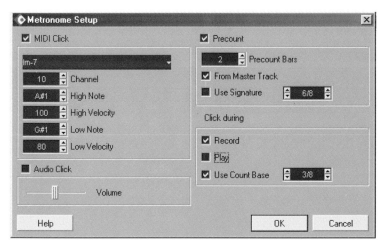

Figure 7.3
Setting up the LM-7 as a Metronome click

Experiment with other devices and sound combinations until you find something that suits you. For example – high-hats mixed with a low audio click (use the volume slider).

Count base settings

In previous versions of Cubase recording in 6/8 time at any tempo above 90 bpm was a frustrating business due to the 'six beats in a bar' click. Now, as any musician knows, 6/8 music has a 'two to the bar' feel – 1 2 3 4 5 6 becomes **1** 2 3 **2** 2 3 – and two beats to the bar is all we want to hear, not six – it doesn't feel right.

Fortunately this can now be done in Cubase by ticking the Use Count Base box in the Metronome Setup, Figure 7.3. When this is activated you can use the field to its right to define a 'rhythm' for the metronome click. It's usually set to 1/4 (suitable for 2/4, 3/4 and 4/4 time signatures) but with a time signature of 6/8 setting it to 3/8 will result in two clicks to the bar. Likewise, a time signature of 12/8 set to a Count Base of 3/8 will result in four clicks to the bar.

Info

You've been working in 4/4 time, your Count Base is set at 1/4 and you switch to a new project in 6/8 time, remember to alter the Count Base to 1/8 (slow) or 3/8 (fast) otherwise you'll hear three clicks to the bar – not want you want at all, Figure 7.3.

Musical or linear time based tracks?

You are given the option of Musical and Linear time based tracks to record on in Cubase and you can switch between them by clicking the musical/linear time base button in the Inspector or Track list, Figure 7.4. But which do you use?

Figure 7.4
Linear (left) and Musical (right) time base buttons

For the majority of conventional music projects you'll be using Musical time based tracks where the events and their time positions are shown as bars, beats and divisions of a beat such as 1/8 notes, 1/16 notes and so on – all very familiar to most musicians.

If you change the tempo of a project the events are played back at an earlier or later point in time and the length of the project will be adjusted accordingly – a faster tempo resulting in a shorter project and a slower tempo resulting in a longer one. All very straightforward stuff – but now for the weird bit.

Change the tracks to a Linear time base and something more difficult to understand happens – the events will be locked to specific time positions and changing the tempo will not alter those positions one jot. How can that be? Well, the fact that MIDI and audio tracks use a musical time base by default and Video and Marker tracks use a linear one gives us a clue.

Video files are shown as events on a Video track with individual frames displayed as thumbnail images, Figure 7.5. This isn't musical material and it can be thought of in terms of seconds or frames per second (fps). A certain group of frames, containing certain certain visual images will appear so many seconds along the time line – they have a Linear time base and cannot be sped up or slowed down (there's no reason to anyway). Linear time based tracks are useful for freezing speech overdubs and sound effects to a particular point in time. Read on...

Figure 7.5
A Video Track

Frozen in time

Suppose you've written some routine background music to accompany a circus video. In addition to the music you have a separate MIDI track, routed to the LM-7 VST Instrument, to record cymbal crashes that coincide with clowns falling over. What happens though, if you decide to increase the tempo of the music slightly? Now you have a problem – the cymbal crashes will play back in the wrong place. The solution? Change the track containing the hits to Linear time. Now you can alter the tempo of the music to your hearts content but the cymbal crashes will not move one jot.

Of course, that's all very well if the music has been recorded on MIDI tracks, but what happens if there are audio tracks as well? They won't fit. Read on…

Stretch to fit

You've increased the tempo of a project but the audio tracks no longer fit the tempo. What do you do? It's easy – just determine in advance what the new speed is going to be and open the Time Stretch dialogue (found in the 'Audio > Process' menu). Select the audio parts and enter the original tempo in the Input section and the new tempo in the Output section. Press 'Process' and the audio will be stretched to fit. Figure 7.6.

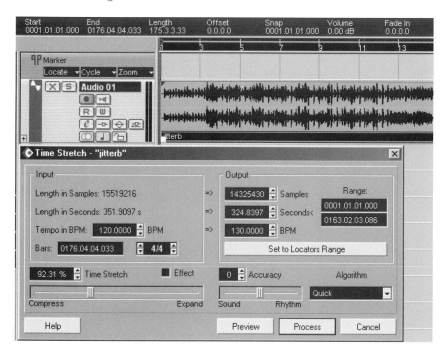

Figure 7.6
Time stretching audio

Crossed time

Strange though it may seem, linear time based tracks can be used for recording music to playback at different tempi simultaneously. For example – you want to cross fade two pieces of music, each containing a different tempo, along with a Video track in the same project. Here's what you do:

Finish the first piece of music and change all the tracks to a linear time base. Enter a new tempo event where the second piece of music will be starting (before the first one finishes). Now write the new piece – on new tracks, of course!

On the beat

If you need to calculate the tempo of an imported audio file, a drum loop perhaps, the Beat Calculator does a reasonable job of it.

First, you home in on one or two bars of the audio, and use Transport > Loop Selection, to loop and play the selection. Then, with Snap turned off, you drag the start and end points of the selection and until you have it just right and the music loops seamlessly (pressing Shift/G will adjust the Locators).

When you're satisfied, open the Beat Calculator (found in the Project menu) and enter the number of encompassed beats in the Beats field. In Figure 7.7 the loop is one bar long and contains four beats. The tempo is calculated and displayed in the BPM field. In Figure 7.7 this is 134 bpm.

Figure 7.7
The loop is one bar long and contains four beats

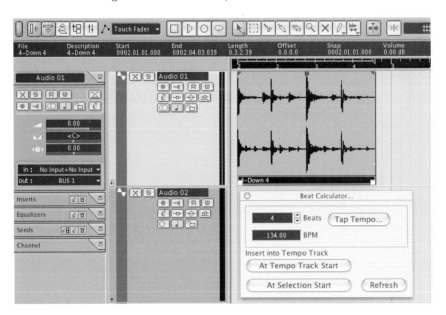

Now insert the loop's tempo into the Tempo track, by clicking one of the buttons in the lower left corner of the Beat Calculator window.

On tap

A quick way to determine the average tempo of freely recorded music is to use the Tap Tempo option in the Beat Calculator. With Playback activated, open the Tap Tempo option and tap along, using the computer spacebar or your mouse. The program calculates the average tempo of the music.

Tapping and mapping

You've recorded a live session in Cubase but the song changes tempo in several places. You want to add a few MIDI tracks – so how do you create a tempo map, that follows the audio? It's easy in v.2 – playback the audio, tap along on your MIDI keyboard and record it to a time based MIDI track. Play the whole thing back, check the results and edit any stray beats. After selecting the events in the Key Editor, open the 'Merge Tempo From Tapping' dialogue (MIDI > Functions). Enter the beat value that you tapped, 1/2, 1/4 or whatever and click OK. The tempo events are inserted into the Tempo Track. Another way…

Tempo mapping with the Time Warp tool

You can create a tempo map from just the drum track of a recording using the Time Warp tool in the Sample Editor. It's slower than using the 'Merge Tempo From Tapping' feature but more accurate.

- First make sure that the very first beat of the recording is placed at the beginning of a bar – let's say bar 1.
- Now locate bar 2, in the ruler, and if it's not there already, drag its position, with the Time Warp tool, to line up with the first drum beat of bar 2.
- Look ahead and locate the next spot where the the audio drifts away from the tempo. Wait! – don't drag the ruler to it just yet. Go back to the beat before it (this one's in sync, right?) Now, hold down the Shift key while clicking with the mouse to insert a tempo event at that point. This ensures that the material to the left will remain unaffected as you make further adjustments along the way.

OK, you can now safely drag the ruler position to line up with the wayward beat. Continue working through the track, matching only the beats that drift from the ruler. But remember – Shift click after matching each beat, to lock the previous material.

Figures 7.8 and 7.9 show a freely recorded drum track before and after tempo matching with the Time Warp tool. Figure 7.10 shows the resulting Tempo Track.

Figure 7.8
A freely recorded drum track, before tempo mapping

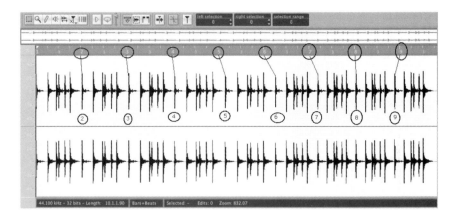

Figure 7.9
The drum track after tempo mapping with the Time Warp tool

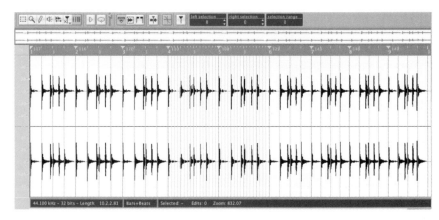

Figure 7.10
The resulting Tempo Track

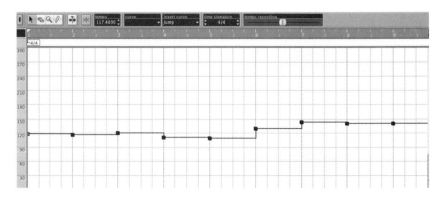

But what if you've recorded a solo piano part on a MIDI track, that drifts in and out of tempo? Again, you can use the Time Warp tool to create a tempo map, only this time use the Key Editor. The procedure is similar to using it in the Sample Editor but you don't have to worry about inserting the tempo events – they're inserted automatically.

Version 2 saw the introduction of the Time Warp tool, Figure 7.11. You use it to drag a musical position (tempo related) and match it to a position in linear time (clock related), Figure 7.12. This makes tasks such as matching sound and picture or creating a tempo map from freely recorded audio and MIDI material, much easier than it ever was in previous versions of Cubase. Tempo events can be inserted into the Tempo Track by holding down the Shift key and clicking with the mouse.

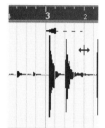

Figure 7.11 (left)
The Time Warp tool

Figure 7,12
You use the Time Warp tool to match musical positions (tempo related) to positions in linear time (clock related).

Time warp tips

To speed things up when tempo mapping, try using the Merge Tempo From Tapping feature first. Then, when the tempo map is complete, fine tune it with the Time Warp tool.

Define a range, with the Range tool, before you use the Time Warp tool and the tempo events outside of that range will remain unaffected.

You don't necessarily have to match the downbeats when tempo mapping from a drum track with the Time Warp tool. Off-beats are just as good, or in fact any obviously significant hit.

Transfers

The facility for importing and exporting tempo maps, lost in v.1 has been revived in v.2. If you want to export a Tempo Track for use in another project, perhaps for music to video, you can save it's information as a special XML file. You can also import a Tempo track but of course, it replaces the one you're already using.

As time slides by

Tools for drawing tempo data have become standard fare in most sequencing packages but not the facility to record tempo changes 'on the fly' by dragging with the mouse. After all, it's much easier to make subtle changes this way. Last seen in Cubase 5, this feature has popped up again in SX/SL 2. All you do now is start playback and adjust a slider to record natural sounding tempo changes into the Tempo track, Figure 7.13.

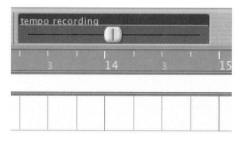

Figure 7.13
You can record 'on the fly' tempo changes using the tempo record slider

Inspector tips

The Inspector can be confusing to the newcomer. What's displayed varies depending on whether a MIDI or audio track is selected, Figures 8.1 and 8.2.

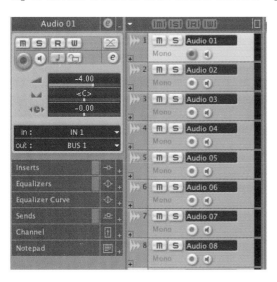

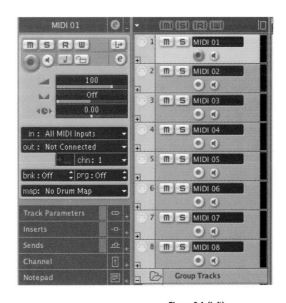

The sections for an audio track, in descending order are:

- The main Inspector.
- Inserts – 8 slots (SX) 5 slots (SL).
- Equalizers – hi, hi mid, lo mid, lo.
- Equalizer Curve.
- Sends – 8 slots (SX) 5 slots (SL).
- Channel – channel strip and fader.
- Notepad (v.2 only).

Figure 8.1 (left)
Audio tracks and the Inspector

Figure 8.2 (right)
MIDI tracks and the Inspector

The sections for a MIDI track, in descending order are:

- The main Inspector.
- Track Parameters.
- Inserts – 4 slots.
- Sends – 4 slots.
- Channel – channel strip and fader.
- Notepad (v2 only).

To have more than one section of the Inspector open, use Ctrl (on the Mac, Command) as you click on the tabs. Using Alt (on the Mac, Option) as you click will open or close all the sections at once.

Multi change

It's tedious changing inputs and outputs, track by track in the Inspector. Press Ctrl, (on the Mac, Command) as you select them on one track, to apply the changes to all tracks. This only applies with MIDI tracks.

Show for me

Figure 8.3
Press this button to show or hide the Inspector

Sometimes having the Inspector displayed is inconvenient. You can show and hide the Inspector using the Show Inspector button, Figure 8.3. Ctrl click (on the Mac, Command clicking) an Inspector tab to bring a hidden section into view without closing an already open one. Alt click (on the Mac, Option click) to either display all five sections at once or close all open sections.

Alternative mixer

You can mix an entire project without leaving the Project window by using the Inspector (well, almost). Use the Edit buttons for quick access to the Channel Settings window and you're off. What you see varies, depending on whether it's an audio or MIDI track.

- Use the Edit button 'e' on a MIDI track to reveal the MIDI Channel Settings – Mixer Channel, Inserts and Sends, Figure 8.4.
- Use the 'e' button on an audio track to reveal the Channel Settings window with the Mixer Channel Strip, Inserts, Sends and EQ, Figure 8.5.
- Use the 'e' button on a track with a VST Instrument to reveal the VST main panel (v.1). However pressing the 'e' button in v.2 opens the MIDI Channel Settings and you have to press the tiny Edit VST Instrument icon to access the VSTi itself, Figure 8.6.

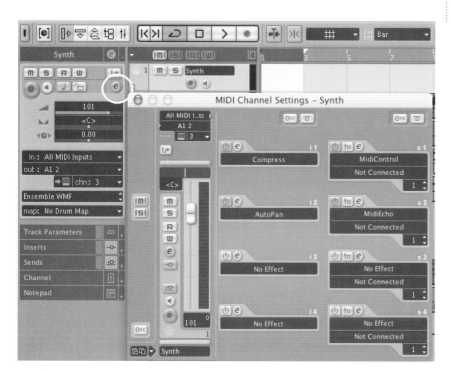

Figure 8.4
On a MIDI track, press 'e' to open the MIDI Channel Settings

Figure 8.5
On an audio track press 'e' to open the Audio Channel Settings

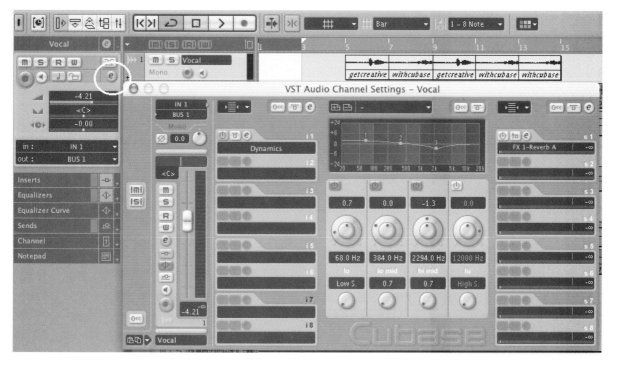

Figure 8.6
Press the Edit VST Instrument button to gain access to the VST Instrument in question

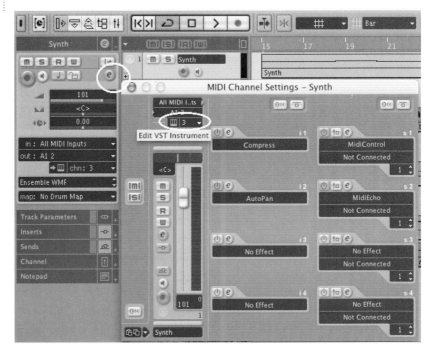

Also under inspection

As well as the usual suspects – audio and MIDI tracks – you can scrutinise Folder tracks in the Inspector too. A list of tracks contained within the folder appear. Click on their icons to reveal an Inspector view with all the usual parameters for that track, Figure 8.7.

Figure 8.7
The baritone sax track is highlighted within a folder and its parameters are revealed in the Inspector

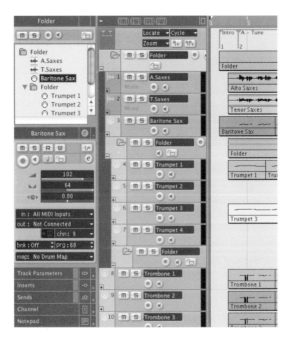

Marker tracks also show up in the Inspector with a list of Markers and their positions, Figure 8.8. You can edit this list here too.

Figure 8.8
You can examine Marker tracks in the Inspector – note: the Info line also contains specific marker data

Auditioning MIDI instruments

Auditioning sounds on your MIDI tracks is so easy when using the Inspector. Click in the centre of the Program Settings and a menu appears containing the patch names of your instrument. Play a track and you can hear the program change in real time as you flick through the menu, Figure 8.9.

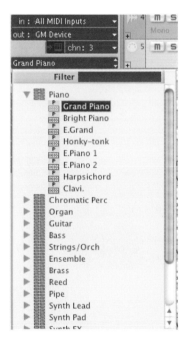

Figure 8.9
You can audition patch changes in real time, as you play the tracks

Transform your playing

A great Cubase feature is the Input Transformer, Figure 8.10. It's a real time version of the Logical Editor. Basically, it enables you to filter out and alter the incoming MIDI data before it's actually recorded. In other words, you will hear the changes as you play. What's the point? Well you could turn a foot pedal controller into a MIDI kick drum for example and play it with your feet, or set up a split keyboard with a different sound for each hand. Open it by using the button in the top right corner of the Inspector, Figure 8.11.

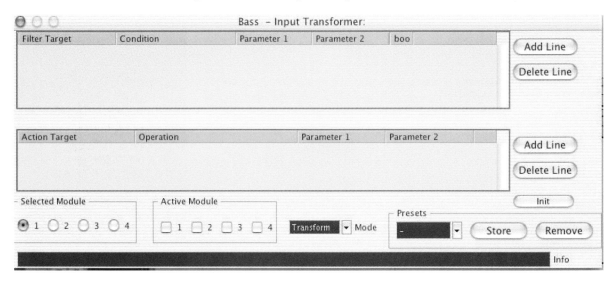

Figure 8.10
You can alter incoming MIDI data in real time with the Transformer

Figure 8.11 (left)
Press the button in the top right corner of the Inspector to access the Transformer

Info

You can't turn off the Transformer by just closing it – you have to deactivate its modules first.

Tip

The Transformer is a real time version of the Logical Editor, covered in chapter 13. Get to grips with the Logical Editor first and you'll find the Transformer easy to understand – see Chapter 13.

Hidden extras

Need extra track parameters? In the Inserts section of the Inspector select Track FX from the pop-up menu. Hey Presto, another set. 'Not much use,' you're probably thinking. Not so – it's handy if you need extra Random Settings for example.

It also contains another feature, that not a lot of people seem to know about, called Scale Transpose, Figure 8.12. All MIDI notes passing through Scale Transpose are transposed to fit a selected scale and key. There are 21 to choose from ranging from straightforward majors and minors to exotic far eastern varieties such as Balinese. Now, route some of your music through it and listen to the result. Well, it works sometimes! Use it experimentally.

Figure 8.12
You can choose from 21 scales in Scale Transpose

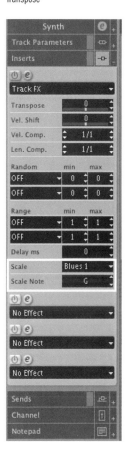

Quick tip

If you're stuck for musical ideas try using the Scale Transpose feature. Put a melody line through the Hungarian scale, for example, and your tune could take off in a completely new direction!

The long and the short

Use the Length Compression feature in the Parameters section of the Inspector to experiment with the length of notes on a particular MIDI track, Figure 8.13. It works in a similar fashion to compression and is applied to the entire track.

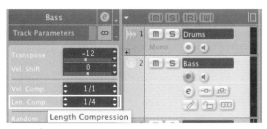

Figure 8.13
Fretless bass notes are shortened using 1/4 Length Compression

You may, for example, have recorded a bass part with a fretless bass patch using fairly long notes. You then decide that a pick bass would be more suitable. There's no need to record it all over again. Apply 1/4 to make all the notes a quarter of their true length. The same thing works in reverse. Enter 4/1 to make the notes play back four times as long as they actually are.

Decisions, decisions

A frequently asked question: When editing MIDI tracks, should I use the Inspector track parameters or the MIDI menu functions?

Answer: Well, it depends on whether you need a permanent alteration or a temporary one. If you're experimenting use the track parameters because any changes you make there are in real time. Bear in mind that they affect the entire track and will not be reflected in the editors. You can make them permanent though, by using the Merge MIDI in Loop function. If you need to make specific changes to parts or events then use the functions. These are permanent – unless you undo them, of course – and will be reflected in the editors.

Key Editor tips

Colouring in

There may be times when you need to work on several parts on different tracks at once in either the Key or List editors. Finding the notes you want to edit is easy using the Colors pop-up menu on the toolbar. Select 'Part' from the pop-up menu. Click on a note and all the corresponding notes in that part will be highlighted in the part's colour – providing that you've coloured the parts in the Project window in the first place of course! Figure 9.1.

Velocity values

Make use of the Insert Velocity feature, found on the toolbar, to determine the velocity you require when you're entering notes with the mouse. In version 1 it's a matter of scrolling the values. In version 2 it's much easier because a Setup box was added where you can define five different velocity levels, Figure 9.2.

Even with five different levels to choose from, it's likely that the end result will sound a little stiff. However, you can soon fix that using the Random feature, in the Track Parameters.

Figure 9.1
Use the Colors pop-up menu on the toolbar to find notes of the same pitch, channel and velocity value as well as notes belonging to selected parts

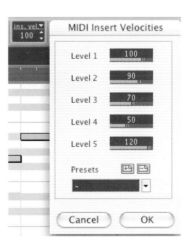

Figure 9.2
You can have five levels of Insert Velocity values

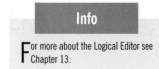

For more about the Logical Editor see Chapter 13.

Alternatively go to MIDI > Logical Presets > experimental > standard set 1 > random velocity (60 – 100). Those velocity values not right for your project? Well, now's your chance to get familiar with the Logical Editor. Open it from the MIDI menu and choose the same preset. Now you can customise the velocity values to suit you.

Getting around

Selecting notes is far easier and much quicker when you use the computer keyboard. Here are a few tips:

* Use the right and left cursor keys to move from event to event.
* Hold down the shift key and use the right and left cursor keys to select a group of events.
* Use the Ctrl and Alt keys (on the Mac, Command and Option) in conjunction with the cursor keys to alter the lengths of selected notes. Ctrl affects the beginnings of a note, Alt the ends.
* Use the up and down cursor keys to transpose selected notes up or down in semitone steps. Holding down shift at the same time will move them in octave steps.
* Hold down Ctrl (on a Mac, Command) whilst clicking a note on the virtual keyboard to select all the notes of the same pitch, Figure 9.3.

Figure 9.3
Selecting notes of the same pitch

Get the habit

Get into the habit of opening the Key Editor, from the Project window. Use Ctrl+E (on the Mac, Command+E). It's much faster than using the menu. Alternatively, double click on the event. This works only when 'Open Key Editor' has been chosen as the Default Edit Action in the Preferences (Event Display > MIDI section). Press Enter to close it.

Tonic Sol-Fa

If you're a singer not used to reading conventional music notation why not display your note events as Tonic Sol-Fa? Go to the Preferences and in the Event Display MIDI section choose 'DoREMi' from the Note Name Style pop-up menu. Now all the note events will show up as Do, Re, Mi etc., Figure 9.4. Use the Color pop-up in the Key Editor toolbar for even easier note recognition.

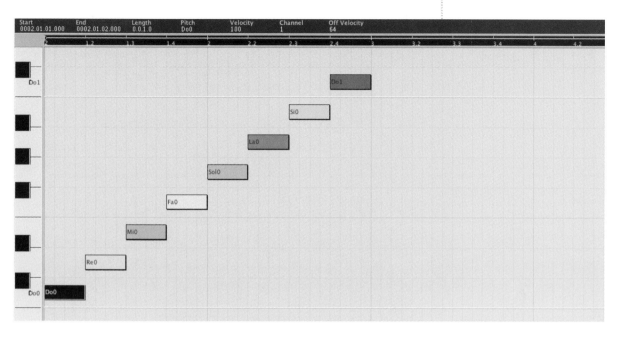

Figure 9.4 (above)
Note events can be displayed as Tonic Sol-Fa

Figure 9.5 (left)
Choose your note name display type in the Preferences section

Info

Various note name options are available in the Note Name Style pop-up menu (Preferences > Event Display > MIDI) including MIDI and Value, Classic, Classic German and DoREMi, Figure 9.5.

Easy piano

You can't play the piano keyboard very well? No problem. Enter the notes using Step Input. What's that? Well, people often wonder what the 'foot' icon on the toolbar is for (in version 2 the foot icon was changed to a staircase, Figure 9.6). If you're amongst them, follow these steps to find out:

Figure 9.6
The Step Input buttons – the 'foot' icon has been replaced by a staircase in SX 2

1 In the Project window, select a Quantize vale of 1/8 Note, turn on Snap and set the Locators to encompass a few bars.
2 Between the Locators, double click on a MIDI track to create an empty part.
3 Set the track output to play back a piano sound.
4 Select the part and use Ctrl+E (on the Mac, Command+E) to open the Key Editor.

5 Click on the Step Input button on the toolbar (staircase or foot). It turns blue along with the Record Pitch and Record NoteOn Velocity buttons, Figure 9.6. A blue line also appears on the screen. This indicates the position where notes are to be entered.

6 Use the right and left cursor keys to scroll the blue line back to the beginning – if it's not there already.

7 Now, play these notes, one by one, on your MIDI keyboard: C3, D3, E3. It doesn't matter if you play out of time. The result should look like Figure 9.7. Play them back.

8 On the toolbar, select a Quantize value of 1/2 Note and ensure that the Length Quantize value displays 'Linked to Quantize'.

9 Set the blue line to where you left off and play this chord: C3, E3, G3 (C major). The result should look like Figure 9.8. Play it back. Easy isn't it?

Figure 9.7
Step entered notes

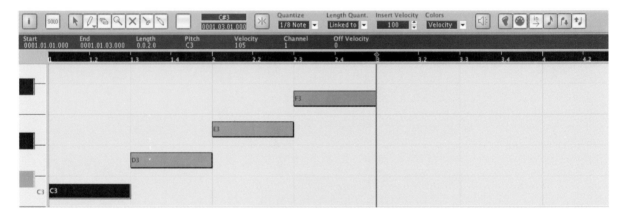

Figure 9.8
Step entered chord

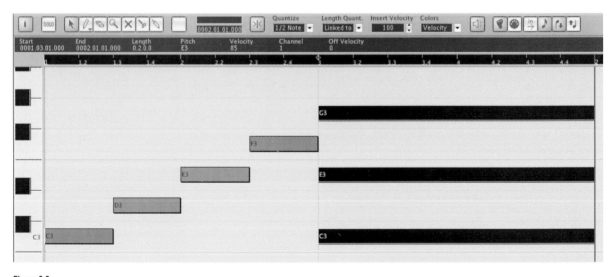

You can step input entire piano parts this way as well as any other type of instrument. Adjust the Quantize or Length Quantize values as you go along, to change the timing and note lengths.

A few more tips:

- Activate Insert mode, (third button from the left in Figure 9.6), to move all notes to the right of the step input position (the blue line) making space for newly inserted notes.
- Press the right cursor key on your computer keyboard to insert rests.
- Click anywhere in the note display to move the step input position manually.

Easy note editing

Okay, you now know what the 'foot' (or 'staircase') is for but are you familiar with the button next to it that looks like a MIDI plug? It's the MIDI Input button. Use it is a fast and intuitive way to edit recorded notes in all the MIDI editors. Here's how it works:

- Record a few notes on a MIDI track and open the Key Editor.
- Click on the MIDI Input button on the toolbar – the 'MIDI plug'. It turns blue and activates the Record Pitch and Record NoteOn Velocity buttons, to its right Figure 9.6.
- Select the first note you played. Now, if you play the same note on the keyboard either harder or softer, the note's velocity will be changed to reflect this. If you play a different note, say a tone higher, the note will be transposed. You'll have noticed that each time a note is edited the cursor moves on to the next note automatically. If you're not happy with the edit, just cursor back and redo it.

The beauty of editing this way is that you can actually hear the notes whilst doing so and thereby adjust your keyboard action accordingly.

Do the splits

In all likelihood you probably split your notes with the Scissors tool. And why not? With a quantize grid value down to 1/64 it's an easy business, with snap activated. However, there may be times when you need even more precision. Select the note(s) and position the project cursor at the exact edit point and use Edit > Split at Cursor. Alternatively press Alt+X (on the Mac, Option+X). This method overrides the snap value.

Another way. Set up the right and left Locators at the split points and use Edit > Split Loop.

Sweeping changes

Make full use of the Controller lane at the bottom of the Key Editor window. You can make sweeping changes to this colourful data display with just a single stroke of the Pencil tool. Here are some of the most useful things you can do here.

In the Controller lane, use the Pencil tool:

Quick tip

Step Input is particularly useful for entering parts for use with Steinberg's Virtual Guitarist plug-in because all the notes and chords line up nicely, end to end. This helps to avoid the drop out that sometimes occurs between chords played on the keyboard.

Info

Step and MIDI Input provide a quick way of inputting and editing notes in all the MIDI editors, not just the Key Editor.

Quick tip

To split chords quickly, select all the notes first before you slice them with the Scissors tool.

- In Draw mode to edit single note velocities.
- In Draw and Paint mode to draw velocity curves, Figure 9.9.
- In Line mode to create velocity ramps (straight lines), Figure 9.10.
- In Draw or Paint mode to create controller events.
- In Draw and Paint mode to draw controller curves, Figure 9.11.
- In Line mode to create controller ramps (straight lines), Figure 9.12.

Figure 9.9
Velocity curves

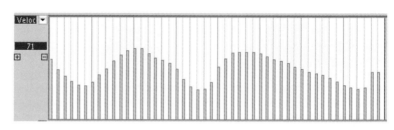

Figure 9.10
Velocity ramp

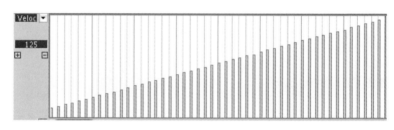

Figure 9.11
Controller curves

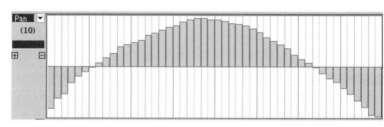

Figure 9.12
Controller ramp

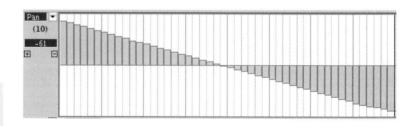

Quick tip

Press or release the Alt key (on the Mac, Option) whilst drawing with the Pencil tool to automatically switch between edit and create modes.

Express yourself

You can use the Controller lane as an extra mixer. For example: Imagine you've sequenced a brass section on a MIDI track. The brass section parts contain sforzando hits – notes that suddenly die and swell very quickly to a climax. That presents a potential nightmare situation when it comes to mixing with lots of jerky fader movements. The solution?

1 Draw and adjust the individual instrument's dynamic hits and swells using Controller No. 11 – Expression (as opposed to Volume) in the Controller lane, Figure 9.13.
2 Adjust the overall track volume levels – in relation to the other instruments, the rhythm section an so on – in the main Mixer. You can also do this in the Project window using the Inspector or automation tracks, Figure 9.14.

Doing it this way gives you the freedom to raise or lower the brass in the mix without upsetting the internal dynamic changes. They've all been taken care of with the expression controller. This is particularly useful if you intend to export your mix as a MIDI file, for use on another computer. In fact professional MIDI file programmers use volume and expression like this all the time.

Figure 9.13
Sforzando trumpet hits drawn with Controller No.11 – Expression

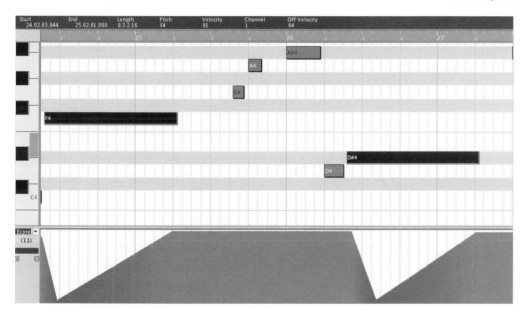

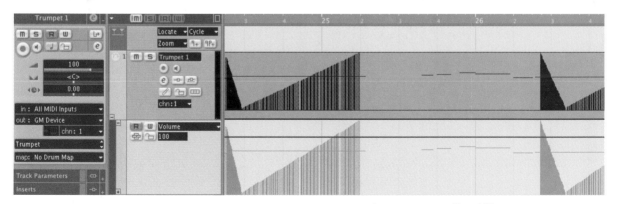

Figure 9.14
Trumpet Master Volume set to 100

If you've ever bought a professionally programmed MIDI file, dig it out, import it into Cubase SX/SL and have a look at the data. The chances are that all the volume levels are set at 100 and the dynamic changes have been assigned to expression. This gives the end user the opportunity to alter the mix without ruining the musical content.

You must have noticed the other Pencil tool drawing modes by now. They are:

- Parabola mode – use it to draw natural shaped velocity and controller curves, Figure 9.15.
- Sine, Triangle and Square modes – use them to create continuous curves and shapes for special effects. These could take the form of continuous left and right panning, Figure 9.16, or a rhythmic gate effect used with volume or expression, Figure 9.17.

Figure 9.15
Velocity curves drawn in Parabola mode

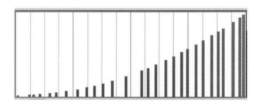

Figure 9.16
Continuous curves drawn in Sine mode – panning

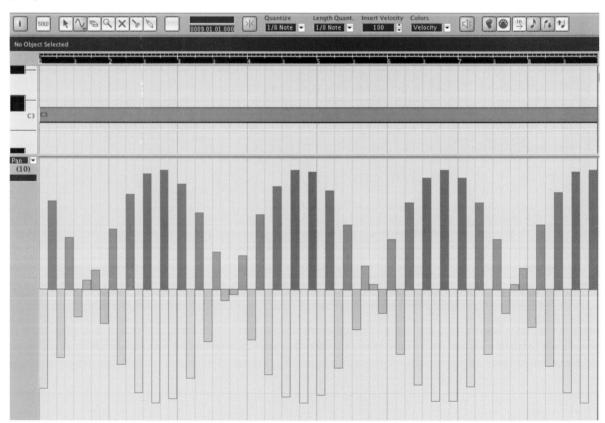

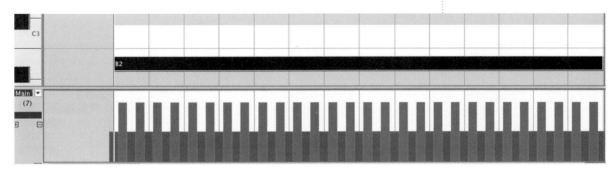

Changing lanes

Need to edit more than one controller in either the Key Editor or Drum Editor at the same time? Right-click in the display area (control and click on a Mac) and select 'Create new controller lane' from the Quick menu to add more lanes .

Hidden controllers

If the controller you need is not on the Key Editor Controller pop-up menu you can add it using the Controller Menu Setup dialogue. Choose 'Setup' from the menu – it's at the bottom. Now you can transfer items from the Hidden list (right) to the menu (left) and vice versa, Figure 9.19.

Figure 9.19
Setting up new controllers

Figure 9.17
Volume gate drawn in Square mode

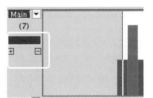

Figure 9.18
Create and remove Controller lanes using these buttons

What's that chord?

Maybe you're still developing your knowledge of music theory. If so, you'll probably find the new chord recognition feature helpful (version 2). It works out chord names for you. As the song cursor moves across a group of notes, the corresponding chord name is instantly displayed in a box on the toolbar – a boon for anybody preparing a chord sheet for the guitarist in the band, Figure 9.20.

Figure 9.20
The chord recognition feature (on the toolbar) works out the names of chords

Figure 9.21
You can set up loops with the Independent Loop feature

Loop back

Remember the independent Loop button in Cubase VST? It's made a welcome return in version 2. Click on the Loop button, on the toolbar and the loop will play independently, while the rest of the project plays merrily away in the background, Figure 9.21. You can define the loop with its own set of locators which show up dark blue in the Ruler or use the numerical fields section, to the right of the Loop button.

All together now

Figure 9.22
Parts List menu and an Edit Active Part Only buttons

Another 'classic' Cubase feature back from the grave in version 2 – the facility to combine multiple parts and edit them together. Of course, you might not be able to fit them all in a single window so a couple of toolbar features have been added – a Parts List menu and an Edit Active Part Only button, Figure 9.22.

You make a part active by selecting it from the pop-up menu or clicking on a note with the arrow tool. Clicking on, and activating the 'Edit Active Part Only' button does just that – restricts editing to the active part only! These features are also available in the List and Drum Editors and audio editors.

Defining borders

Figure 9.23
Part borders defined using the 'Show Part Borders' tool

Another new tool in version 2, the 'Show Part Borders' tool is used to define the borders of an active part and when it's activated, all parts except the active one are greyed out. Two little indicators appear in the ruler, marking its beginning and end. These can be moved about, to alter the size of the actual part itself, Figure 9.23.

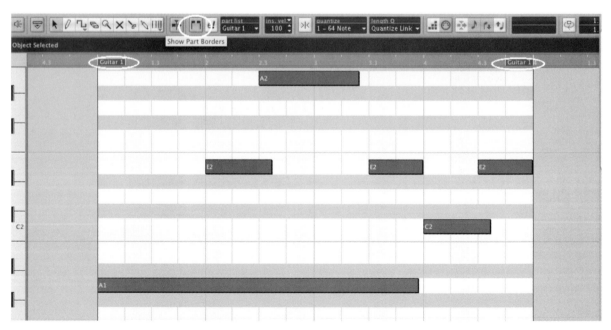

List Editor tips

F is for filter

The List Editor is the best place for detailed MIDI editing in Cubase but many first time users are put off by its apparent complexity. A lengthy string of data can appear very confusing to musicians who are primarily concerned with notes and not numbers.

To clarify things, press the button marked 'F', on the toolbar. A filter bar appears with a row of tick boxes, each one representing a data type. In version 2 the 'F' button is replaced with a rather curious looking symbol depicting an eye, a tick and a cross. Now you can make a complicated list more manageable and hide any unnecessary data from view by ticking the relevant boxes, Figures 10.1 and 10.2.

Filter	☐ Note	☐ Controller	☐ Pitch Bend	☐ Program Change	☐ Aftertouch	☐ Pol

L	Type	Start	End	Length	Data 1	Data 2	Data 3	Chann
	Controller	83.02.02.065			Expression	93		10
	Controller	83.02.02.065			Expression	112		1
	Controller	83.02.02.070			Expression	93		2
	Controller	83.02.02.080			Expression	92		3
	Controller	83.02.02.085			Expression	112		4
	Controller	83.02.02.090			Expression	98		5
	Controller	83.02.02.100			Expression	112		7
	Pitchbend	83.02.02.100			4799			9
	Controller	83.02.02.105			Expression	112		8
	Controller	83.02.02.115			Expression	92		9
♩	Note	83.02.03.000	83.02.04.090	0.0.1.90	A3	83	64	1
♩	Note	83.02.03.000	83.02.04.100	0.0.1.100	A2	84	64	3
♩	Note	83.02.03.005	83.03.01.005	0.0.2.0	C#1	83	64	2
♩	Note	83.02.03.005	83.02.03.015	0.0.0.10	A2	93	64	10
	Pitchbend	83.02.03.015			4220			9
	Controller	83.02.03.030			Expression	111		1
	Controller	83.02.03.030			Expression	92		10
	Pitchbend	83.02.03.035			3144			9
	Controller	83.02.03.035			Expression	92		2
	Controller	83.02.03.045			Expression	91		3
	Controller	83.02.03.050			Expression	111		4
	Controller	83.02.03.060			Expression	97		5
	Pitchbend	83.02.03.060			2068			9
	Controller	83.02.03.065			Expression	111		7
	Controller	83.02.03.075			Expression	111		8
	Pitchbend	83.02.03.080			827			9
	Controller	83.02.03.080			Expression	91		9
	Pitchbend	83.02.03.100			0			9
♩	Note	83.02.03.110	83.03.01.025	0.0.1.35	E3	93	64	9
♩	Note	83.02.04.005	83.03.01.035	0.0.1.30	C#3	93	64	9

Figure 10.1
List Editor displaying Note, Pitch Bend and Controller information

Figure 10.2
List Editor after Controller and Pitch Bend
have been filtered out

L	Type	Start	End	Length	Data 1		Data 2	Data 3	Chan
	Note	85.03.03.000	85.04.02.065	0.0.3.65	D3		82	64	3
	Note	85.03.03.010	85.04.02.055	0.0.3.45	F#3		88	64	3
	Note	85.03.04.000	85.03.04.010	0.0.0.10	D1		95	64	10
	Note	85.03.04.110	85.04.01.000	0.0.0.10	C1		95	64	10
	Note	85.03.04.110	85.04.01.000	0.0.0.10	D1		95	64	10
	Note	85.03.04.115	85.04.02.115	0.0.2.0	G0		90	64	2
	Note	85.04.01.000	85.04.04.115	0.0.3.115	G2		91	64	1
	Note	85.04.01.000	85.04.01.010	0.0.0.10	E2		95	64	10
	Note	85.04.01.115	85.04.02.005	0.0.0.10	A1		95	64	10
	Note	85.04.02.110	85.04.04.035	0.0.1.45	C#3		90	64	3
	Note	85.04.02.115	85.04.04.115	0.0.2.0	E0		93	64	2
	Note	85.04.02.115	85.04.04.030	0.0.1.35	E3		82	64	3
	Note	85.04.03.000	85.04.04.115	0.0.1.115	E4		77	64	1
	Note	85.04.03.000	85.04.03.010	0.0.0.10	E2		95	64	10
	Note	85.04.03.000	85.04.04.115	0.0.1.115	G3		76	64	1
	Note	85.04.03.010	85.04.03.020	0.0.0.10	C1		93	64	10
	Note	85.04.03.105	85.04.03.115	0.0.0.10	A1		95	64	10

Behind the mask

Another way to hide specific events is to use the Mask function. For example, if you want to home in on a series of Program Changes in a list and perhaps alter their positions, you first select a single Program Change event in the list itself and then select 'Event Types' from the pop-up Mask menu. The result – all events except Program Changes are hidden from view, Figure 10.3. Various display options are possible and exactly how the Mask function behaves is determined in the pop-up menu.

Figure 10.3
All events in the list, other than Program
changes, are masked

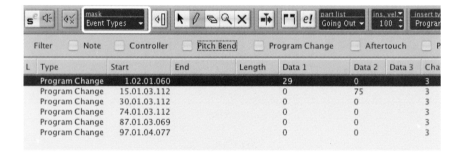

Set-up bars

If you intend exporting your projects as MIDI files, perhaps for use in a program such as Emagic Logic, it's a good idea to create a set-up bar at the beginning of each track containing Program Change, Volume, Expression, Pan and Effect messages. The List Editor is the ideal place to do this. Use the Insert pop-up menu to select a message type and click in the grid area with the Pencil tool to insert it. Now scroll the data to the required values. In version 1 you have to type them in. Because some synths and sound modules are slower than others at reading the set-up messages, set them a few ticks apart, Figure 1.4.

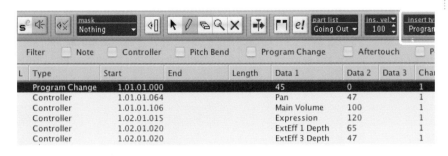

Figure 10.4
A MIDI track set-up bar

Move on up

If you need to move a whole load of data forward, maybe to make way for a set-up measure, select all the data in the List Editor and scroll only the first event. Everything else will move forward as you do so and remain in place, relevant to the first event. This is only possible in version 2.

The hidden editor

System Exclusive events are only partly displayed in the List Editor and you cannot carry out any editing apart from moving their position. However, you can edit them proper by clicking in the Comments column to reveal the System Exclusive Editor, Figure 10.5.

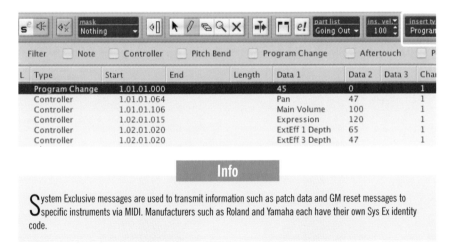

Figure 10.5
Click in the Comments column to open the System Exclusive Editor

Info

System Exclusive messages are used to transmit information such as patch data and GM reset messages to specific instruments via MIDI. Manufacturers such as Roland and Yamaha each have their own Sys Ex identity code.

Score Editor tips

A lot of people give the Score Editor a wide berth, because they don't read music. And that's fine because all the MIDI editing in a project can be done in the Key, List and Drum Editors, without ever opening the Score Editor. However, if you're a musician who reads the dots you'll very likely feel more comfortable working in the Score Editor. For you, reading notes on the staff will probably be easier than reading events on a piano roll grid.

Even if you don't read music very well, the Score Editor can be very useful. For example - you've recorded a MIDI brass or string part but it doesn't sound very realistic. You may decide to have a friend play the part for real and record their performance on an audio track. But how do you tell them what to play? Of course, you can always play the MIDI part over and over and have them learn it 'by ear'. A much quicker way would be to give them the music to read. After all, it's all there in the Score Editor, ready to be printed out. But you can't just open the Score Editor and press the 'print' button for the best results. You might need a few tips. Read on…

Page or Edit mode

Once you've opened the Score Editor you can toggle the display between Page and Edit mode (Score > Edit/Page). But which one do you use? If you're editing the MIDI data, as an alternative to the Key Editor, use the Edit Mode, Figure 11.1. The score scrolls according to the project cursor and the music is more widely spaced and easier to edit.

Figure 11.1
Score Editor in Edit mode

Info

The Score Editor section of Cubase varies considerably between Cubase SL and Cubase SX. Basically, the SL version is limited in its layout and printing facilities. For serious layout and printing you''ll need the SX version.

But if you're preparing a score for printing use the Page mode, Figure 11.2. You can do everything here that you can do in Edit mode but you also gain access to the special layout tools. Also, the screen now represents a page of manuscript paper, complete with horizontal and vertical rulers - like in a desktop publishing program.

Figure 11.1
Score Editor in Page mode

Destructive behaviour

When you're preparing a score for printing, just altering the display parameters is not always enough to achieve a coherent score. Sometimes you'll have to go a stage further and alter the actual lengths and positions of the notes themselves. Of course, doing this will destroy the playback of your music. To avoid this happening, before you do any layout work in the Score Editor, always make a second copy to work on. That way your original masterpiece remains intact.

The special relationship

It's important to understand the relationship between the Score Editor and the rest of the program. To begin with, you can't display the notes of recorded audio data. Not for the time being anyway. Maybe one day the technology will be able to handle it. So, for the foreseeable future at least, you will only be able to see recorded MIDI data in the Score Editor, displayed as conventional music notation, according to the settings you make.

Before editing, every note you record as MIDI data in Cubase is faithfully displayed in the Score Editor exactly as you played it. For example four bars of Jingle Bells captured in Cubase might look like this, Figure 11.3. Looks wrong, doesn't it? But if you were to play it through, it would probably sound fine. However, to get it to look correct as well, you would have to change a few settings in the Staff Settings dialogue, Figures 11.4 and 11.5. You see, the MIDI data itself doesn't change - just the interpretation.

Figure 11.3
Jingle Bells before Staff Settings applied

Figure 11.4
The first step to a clean score – the Staff Settings

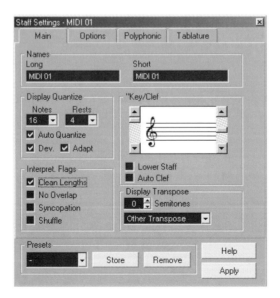

Figure 11.5
Jingle Bells after Staff Settings applied

Quick cleanup

Cubase does a pretty good job of interpreting MIDI data straight away but in most cases it needs a little help from you. You can clean up your scores quickly by telling Cubase how you want things displayed using the Staff Settings box, Figure 11.4. Work through each staff in turn, giving each one it's own settings.

After selecting a staff, begin the cleanup in the Display Quantize section. If the smallest note recorded on this track was a 1/16 note, choose that value in the Note pop-up field. If the smallest note recorded on this track was a 1/8 note, choose that value in the Note pop-up field. You get the idea? To avoid having unnecessary rests all over the place, the best value to enter in the Rest field is usually 4. A setting that works well with most music is 'Note 1/16 and Rest 4'. Of course, if the music contains triplets use the values with the T appendage, 1/8T, 1/16T and so on.

If the music contains a mixture of triplets and straight note values tick the Auto Quantize box. If not leave it blanked out. Two further boxes, Dev and Adapt only appear when the Auto Quantize box is ticked and help further with the cleaning up of freely played notes, not dead on the beat.

Next, move to the Interpretation Flags section. If you played chords they'll probably have different note lengths (it's unlikely that all your fingers left the keyboard at precisely the same time) and ticking the Clean Lengths box will display them properly, Figures 11.6 and 11.7.

Figure 11.6
Chords before Clean Lengths applied

Figure 11.7
Chords after Clean Lengths applied

When you play legato phrases on a keyboard (flowing string lines for example) overlapping notes are inevitable and result in a messy score display. You can clean these up by ticking the No Overlap box. Figures 11.8 and 11.9 show a line with overlapping notes, in the Key Editor, and the Score Editor both before and after the No Overlap feature has been activated.

Figure 11.8
Overlapping notes

Figure 11.9
Overlapping notes cleaned up with 'No Overlap' ticked in the Staff Settings

If you played something jazzy, with a swing feel, some of the notes will probably lie across the beat. This is called syncopation. Cubase displays syncopated notes logically with ties across the beat – unless you tell it to do otherwise. To make them easier to read tick the Syncopation box. Figures 11.10 and 11.11 show syncopated notes before and after Syncopation has been activated.

Figure 11.10
Syncopated notes

Figure 11.11
Syncopated notes after 'Syncopation' ticked in the Staff Settings

Jazz quavers

Jazz music is written one way – straight, with even eighth notes – and played another – swingy, with a triplet feel. Of course, Cubase is utterly logical in its interpretation and displays triplets – until you tell it otherwise. Tick the Shuffle box, in the Staff Settings, to display the triplets as ordinary eighth notes which are much easier to read. All you have to do now is instruct the player to reinterpret them with a swing feel.

Using force

Sooner or later you'll probably encounter a group of notes that will refuse to cooperate with the display settings you've made. However, you can force the issue by using the Display Quantize tool. Select it and up pops the Display Quantize box, Figure 11.12. Enter the required settings and with the Quantize tool click on the score at the exact spot that the rogue notes begin. Use the mouse position display for pinpoint accuracy.

Figure 11.12
Use the Display Quantize tool to force notes to obey the rules!

The last resort

Sometimes even the Display Quantize tool will fail to deal with a particularly awkward group of notes. If that case you'll have to change the notes themselves. Of course, this will alter the playback. What's that – you didn't make a backup?

Tip

If you use the Score Editor for most of your editing you might like to make it your default Editor. Use the Default Edit Action pop-up menu in the Preferences section (Event Display > MIDI).

No notes

It frequently happens: You open the Score Editor and all you can see are the note stems and beams. Everything else is has been greyed out. What do you do? Open the Toolstrip and turn on one or all of the layers. There are three layers and which score attributes are assigned to which layer can be set using Scores > Event Layer in the Preferences section, Figure 11.13.

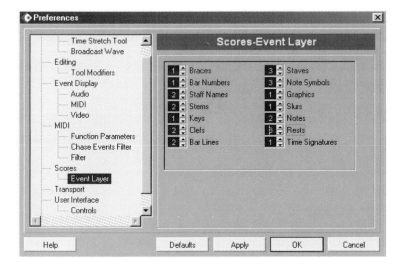

Figure 11.13
Score attributes can be assigned to one of three different layers

Garbled score

Another common scenario: You open up the Score Editor and instead of notes all you can see are strange symbols, telephones and the like. What do you do? On the PC, go to Control Panel > Fonts and press Ctrl – A, to select all the fonts. Close the window and that should be that. It doesn't seem to happen on the Mac, but if it does, presumably you go to Macintosh HD > Library > Fonts, and do the same.

Tip

Isn't it annoying, when you're transposing a note and it suddenly jumps on to the staff above or below? To prevent this happening turn on the Lock symbol – 'L' – on the Toolstrip. You can also lock layers this way ('L' – layer buttons).

Jumpin' and scrollin'

If you're working on a score with several instruments you can jump from staff to staff by using the up and down arrow keys on your keypad. The left and right arrows can then be used to scroll to the notes you want to edit.

All together now

You might want to select a group of notes on the same stem (a chord), perhaps to lengthen them all together. Select the bottom note, hold down Shift and use the right arrow key to cursor up. Or select the top note, hold Shift and use the left arrow key to cursor down. Once selected change their lengths in the Info line.

Quick clicks

- You can enter key changes on more than one staff at a time. Hold down the Alt key (on the Mac, Option) while you enter the key change with the Pencil tool.
- You can move notes sideways without altering their pitch. Hold down Ctrl (on the Mac, Command) as you do so.
- Double click on a note to open the Set Note Info box, Figure 11.14. You can use this to change note-heads, set tablature, change stem directions, hide stems and so on. The box floats while you work your way around the score.
- Double click in the white area, to the left of a staff, to open the Staff Settings box.

Figure 11.14
You can change note heads and stems using the Set Note Info box

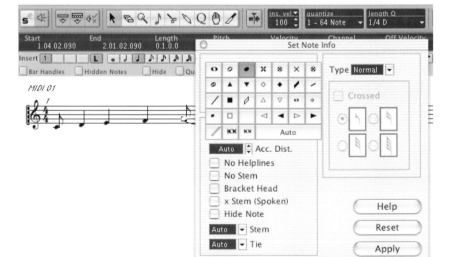

A touch of style

Having the first staff of a music part indented a little to the right looks stylish, Figure 11.15. Select the first bar line, press Shift and drag it with the Arrow tool. Of course, you can move other bars this way too. Remember though – it's a layout feature and only works in Page Mode.

Trumpet 1

Figure 11.15
It's stylish to indent the first staff of a
musician's part

Do the splits

If you've recorded a piano part on a single track, all the notes will be displayed on a single staff – not what you want when it's printed out. To overcome this problem, you need create a split point. Open the Staff Settings box and select 'Split' in the Staff Mode pop-up and choose a value in the Splitpoint field. The split point is set to a default value of C3, (okay in many cases) but you might have to experiment with other values to get things looking correct.

Transposing instruments

For many instruments, just printing out parts in the written key will not do. For example – you sequence a part for the alto saxophone in the key of C, print it out and give it to a real saxophone player to perform. He'll probably take a quick look at it and, if he's a polite kind of guy, hand it back. (If he's not so polite, he'll probably throw it in the bin). Why? Because when you play middle C on the piano an alto saxophone plays the A above middle C. This is because the alto saxophone is a transposing instrument and is pitched in Eb (Eb on the piano is C on the alto saxophone). Now, if this all seems too complicated, don't worry because Cubase works out the transposition for you so…

   If you have a part that is to be printed out for a transposing instrument – trumpet, alto sax and so on – open the Staff Settings box and choose the instrument in the Display Transpose pop-up. Press 'Apply' and the score will be instantly transposed, complete with a new key signature. The degree of transposition is shown just above, as semitones.

Fast entry

If you enter notes manually onto the score, using a mouse, you'll know that selecting a Quantize value helps position the notes correctly on the screen. You'll also know that frequently changing the Quantize value is a bit of a pain in the butt. It's faster and easier if you assign a key command to each value. Go to the Key Commands dialogue on the File menu an set them up in the MIDI Quantize folder.

Keeping tabs

You've sequenced a part for the guitar player in your band but he doesn't read music. No worries. Open the Staff Settings and select Tablature, Figures 11.16 and 11.17. Select 'Guitar' in the Instrument pop-up and tick the Tablature Mode box and click 'Apply' for instant tablature.

Figure 11.16
Guitar part

Figure 11.17
Guitar part displayed as tablature

Drum track tips

Drum Editor v Key Editor

After recording drums on a MIDI track you'll most likely want to edit them. Now, you could use the Key Editor but finding individual drum sounds might prove confusing unless you can remember the exact key mapping. A better way is to use the Drum Editor where all the drums are individually listed in a column and the beats are displayed on a grid. It works in much the same way as the Key Editor but has been optimised for drums. For example – apart from the usual facility to solo the track there's an extra button (Drum Solo) for soloing individual drum sounds.

No drum tracks?

We used to have dedicated drum tracks in previous versions of Cubase and pressing Ctrl+D on the keyboard used to open the Drum Editor. Not anymore. There's no keystroke command for accessing the Drum Editor from the within Project window at all but if a Drum Map has been selected in the Inspector, pressing Ctrl+E (on the Mac, Command+E) will open it, instead of the usual Key Editor. In effect, having the Drum Map selected for a MIDI track turns it into a drum track, Figure 12.1.

Figure 12.1
Drum map selected

Map reading

If 'No Drum Map' is selected in the Drum Editor pop-up menu only three columns are displayed – Pitch, Instrument and Quantize, Figure 12.2.

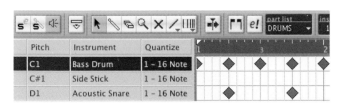

Figure 12.2
Only three columns are shown in the Drum Editor if 'No Drum Map' is selected in the Inspector

These days most budget sound cards include a GM sound set and the basic drum sound names (shown by default) in the Instrument column are all that many of you will need to write and edit drum parts. Even if your card wasn't bundled with MIDI sounds, the chances are that you are using a hardware GM sound module or synth of some kind. If on the other hand you are using an older synthesiser or a dedicated drum machine then you'll probably need to get to grips with the dreaded Drum Map.

A good way to get started with drum maps is to load a project and view the drums in the Drum Editor using a GM Map. Select the GM map from the pop-up, in the lower left corner of the Drum Editor, Figure 12.3.

Figure12.3
GM Drum map selected in the Drum Editor

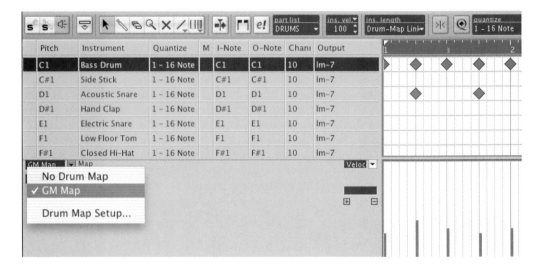

Here's a quick run down of the column parameters and what they do:

- Pitch – A note number links notes on a MIDI track to drum sounds. In the GM Map C1 is mapped to a Bass Drum, D1 is mapped to an Acoustic Snare and so on).
- Instrument – The name of the drum.
- Quantize – This value is used when entering notes on the grid. You can use different values for different drums.
- Mute – Mutes a drum.
- I-note – The actual note you either play or enter with the Drumstick tool (the input note).
- O-note – The actual note (drum) that's played back after mapping (the output note).
- Channel – The drum is played back on this MIDI channel.
- Output – The drum is played back on this MIDI output.

'Very interesting', I hear you say, 'but what's the point of all this'. Well, the two most important parameters in the list – as far as mapping drums is concerned – are the I-notes and the O-notes. In the standard GM Drum Map they are all the same – play C1 on a MIDI keyboard (the I-note) and you hear a bass drum, C1 (the O-note). Now suppose you had to play the Bass Drum (C1), various Bongoes (C3 – E3) and Claves (D#4), on a Latin style track. Try it – you have to admit, it's a bit of a stretch to say the least, especially if you're no great shakes on the piano keyboard. The way round the problem? – map the Latin instruments close to the Bass Drum by typing in new I-notes. Now everything will be 'under the fingers' and much easier to play.

A possible scenario – you've created a driving drum track for a rock song using GM sounds as a guide but they're a bit feeble sounding and you decide to play them back using your favourite drum machine. But when you play the track, instead of hearing something akin to John Bonham, the drum machine produces a jumble of unrelated sounds – something like a cross between a gentle Bossa Nova and a Stockhausen composition. What's needed is a drum map.

Map making

Creating drum maps is done in the Drum Map Setup (use the MIDI or pop-up menu to open it), Figure 12.4. It's an exact replica of the Drum Editor sound list and you can still audition the sounds by clicking in the far left column. All you have to do is change the I-notes and O-notes to match those of your own instrument, type in suitable names and press the Assign button. You can also save the newly created map here, for future use.

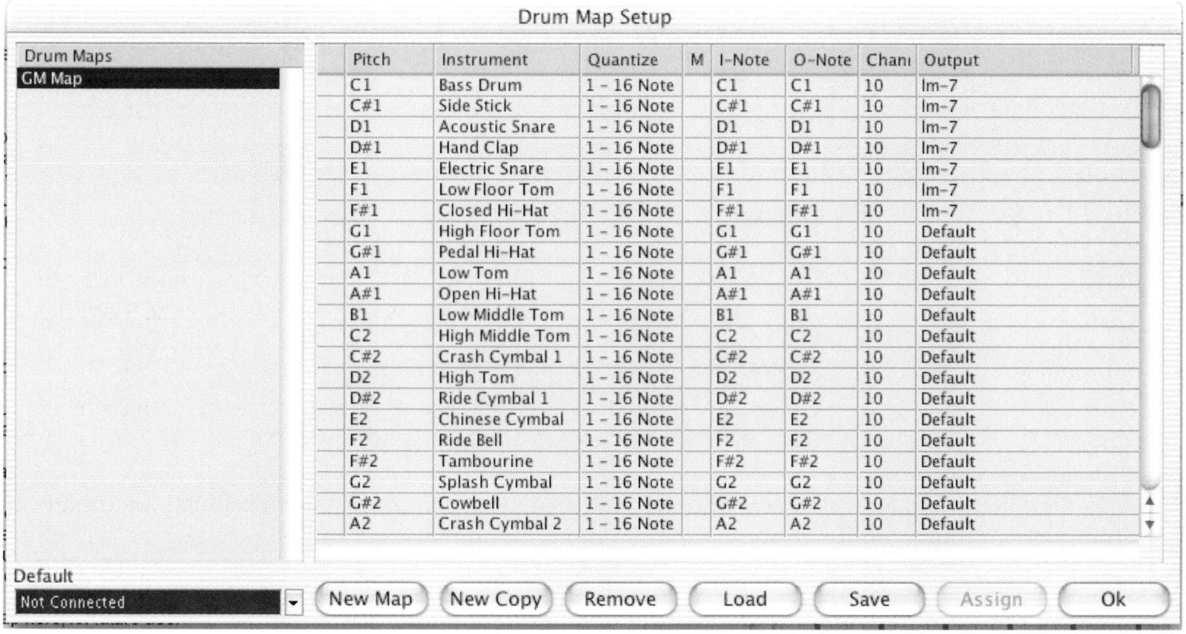

Quick tip

You can change the order of the columns in the Drum Editor by dragging their headings.

Figure 12.4
You can create drum maps in the Drum Map Setup

Drum Map Setup

Drum Maps	Pitch	Instrument	Quantize	M	I-Note	O-Note	Chan	Output
GM Map	C1	Bass Drum	1 – 16 Note		C1	C1	10	Im-7
	C#1	Side Stick	1 – 16 Note		C#1	C#1	10	Im-7
	D1	Acoustic Snare	1 – 16 Note		D1	D1	10	Im-7
	D#1	Hand Clap	1 – 16 Note		D#1	D#1	10	Im-7
	E1	Electric Snare	1 – 16 Note		E1	E1	10	Im-7
	F1	Low Floor Tom	1 – 16 Note		F1	F1	10	Im-7
	F#1	Closed Hi-Hat	1 – 16 Note		F#1	F#1	10	Im-7
	G1	High Floor Tom	1 – 16 Note		G1	G1	10	Default
	G#1	Pedal Hi-Hat	1 – 16 Note		G#1	G#1	10	Default
	A1	Low Tom	1 – 16 Note		A1	A1	10	Default
	A#1	Open Hi-Hat	1 – 16 Note		A#1	A#1	10	Default
	B1	Low Middle Tom	1 – 16 Note		B1	B1	10	Default
	C2	High Middle Tom	1 – 16 Note		C2	C2	10	Default
	C#2	Crash Cymbal 1	1 – 16 Note		C#2	C#2	10	Default
	D2	High Tom	1 – 16 Note		D2	D2	10	Default
	D#2	Ride Cymbal 1	1 – 16 Note		D#2	D#2	10	Default
	E2	Chinese Cymbal	1 – 16 Note		E2	E2	10	Default
	F2	Ride Bell	1 – 16 Note		F2	F2	10	Default
	F#2	Tambourine	1 – 16 Note		F#2	F#2	10	Default
	G2	Splash Cymbal	1 – 16 Note		G2	G2	10	Default
	G#2	Cowbell	1 – 16 Note		G#2	G#2	10	Default
	A2	Crash Cymbal 2	1 – 16 Note		A2	A2	10	Default

Default
Not Connected

(New Map) (New Copy) (Remove) (Load) (Save) (Assign) (Ok)

Before you embark on making your own map, pop the Cubase SX/SL CD into your computer's drive, press the Load button and navigate your way to the Drum maps folder, Figure 12.5. There are dozens of maps to be found there for Alesis, Emu, Kawai, Korg, Roland, Waldorf and Yamaha instruments.

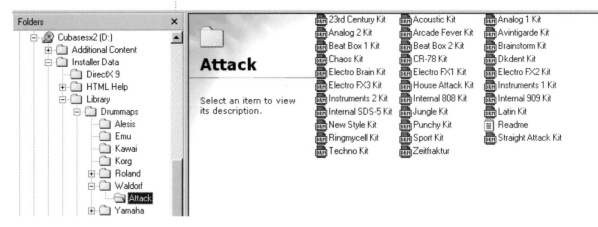

Figure 12.5
You'll find dozens of drum maps on the SX/SL CD

Quick tip

Have a browse about on the Internet – you may find that somebody has already made a drum map for your particular bit of kit.

Exporting MIDI drum tracks

If you have constructed a drum track using a mapped kit and you intend to export it as a MIDI file, for use on another computer or another sequencer program, use the O-note Conversion function found in the MIDI menu. Cubase scans the selected MIDI part(s) and sets the pitch of all the notes to their O-note settings.

Spread the load

You're not restricted to using just one instrument in a Drum Map. For example – if you particularly like the sound of a bass drum in a GM kit and the sound of a snare on your Alesis drum machine and the hi-hats on the Im-7 (VST Instrument, supplied with SX/SL) why not use them all together? Just change the names in the Output column to the names of those instruments, Figure 12.6.

Figure 12.6
Try using different instruments for different drum sounds

Pitch	Instrument	Quantize	M	I-Note	O-Note	Chani	Output
C1	Bass Drum	1 – 16 Note		C1	C1	10	Im–7
C#1	Side Stick	1 – 16 Note		C#1	C#1	10	Model-E
D1	Acoustic Snare	1 – 16 Note		D1	D1	10	HALion
D#1	Hand Clap	1 – 16 Note		D#1	D#1	10	SampleTank2.vsi
E1	Electric Snare	1 – 16 Note		E1	E1	10	GM Device
F1	Low Floor Tom	1 – 16 Note		F1	F1	10	Im–7
F#1	Closed Hi-Hat	1 – 16 Note		F#1	F#1	10	Im–7

Different optimise

Okay, you've mapped the I-notes and O-notes of your instruments and everything is now easy to play and 'under the fingers' but the editing side of things remains a pain due to the wide spread of instrument sounds in the list. This can be easily rectified – just drag the columns up and down to where you want them, as you do the tracks in the Project window.

Quick tip

To select the same MIDI channel or Output for all sounds in a drum map press Ctrl (on a Mac, Command) as you make your selection.

The rubber pencil

A glance at the Drum Editor toolbar shows a slightly different set of tools to those found in the other Editors. For a start there's no Pencil tool. It's been replaced with the Drumstick tool, which is used to enter the drum beats. However, it also serves as a quick eraser, handy for deleting individual events on the grid – just click on an existing beat and it disappears. If you need to delete several events at once then you'll have to resort to the usual methods, selecting events and either pressing the backspace key on your computer or using the Erase tool. There are no Scissors or Glue tube tools in the Drum Editor either, because we don't need them – think about it . . .

Diamonds aren't forever

Some people are baffled by the diamond symbols which are used to display the note positions on the grid and wonder why they can't alter their lengths, particularly when they represent a cymbal crash. The answer is simple – drum sounds are usually single-hit samples. A snare hit will be short and depending on how it was recorded, may include some reverb. The same goes for bass drum hits. Cymbals of course last longer, but they are still represented on the grid as a single hit. Only their starting point, in time, is shown on the grid. Their decay time will be determined by the length of the sample itself.

Getting around

Selecting beats is easy when you use the computer keyboard. Here are a few tips:

- Use the right and left cursor keys to move from event to event.
- Hold down the shift key and use the right and left cursor keys to select a group of events.
- Use the up and down cursor keys to transpose selected beats up or down the grid. Hold down shift at the same time and they will move them 12 places on the grid (an octave).
- Press Shift and double click a beat to select all the following beats using the same sound.

Drum solos

If you want to hear the drums in isolation use the Solo button in the usual way. However, you might want to hear individual drum sounds on their own – to check the accuracy of a hi-hat pattern perhaps. To do this, select the drum sound and then press the Drum Solo button, Figure 12.7. All the other drum sounds will be muted.

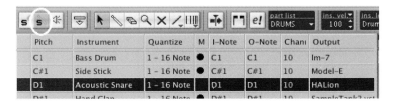

Figure 12.7
Auditioning an individual drum

Speedy entry

Forget the mouse – here's a quick way to enter beats on the grid. Let's say you want a Bass Drum sounding on the first and third beats of the bar (in 4/4 time). Assuming that you're using a GM Drum Map:

1 Enter a beat on the top line of the grid (C1 Bass Drum).
2 Set the value in the Quantize column to 1/4.
3 With the beat selected, press Ctrl+D (on the Mac, Command+D) in rapid succession to duplicate it.

Of course, you can select whole groups of beats and duplicate them in this way. Another fast way to do the same thing – use Step Input:

1 Set the value in the Global Quantize box to 1/4.
2 Activate the Step Input (Press the 'foot' or 'staircase' icon).
3 Use your MIDI keyboard to enter the beats.

The virtual drummer

Many Cubase users prefer to sequence their drum parts by entering the beats with a mouse in the Drum Editor. This is fine for music that relies heavily on drum loops such as dance music. Others prefer to play a 'virtual kit'. Which way it's done depends mainly on the style of music being recorded. To capture the feel and spontaneity of a real drummer it's probably best to play the part first using a MIDI keyboard and edit it afterwards in one of the Editors. If a repetitive loop is needed, step entry may be the way to go.

Here are a few pointers when recording 'live style' drums:

- People new to song writing and sequencing often spend hours perfecting a drum track before they even think about recording anything else. Quite often, it has to be scrapped anyway, at a later stage, because it doesn't fit the bass part which was influenced by the guitar rhythm which was influenced by the melody and so on. A better bet is to record some melodic material first. Once the melody and bass are down it's much easier to be a 'virtual drummer' and instil some spontaneity and feel into the music.
- If possible record in stretches of eight bars or so at a time. This helps create a natural flow and is preferable to cutting and pasting one or two bar segments.
- Drum rolls are best sequenced by step entry. It's no easy matter to roll two fingers as fast as two drum sticks. Use the Drum Editor.
- Try playing the kick and snare drums first and overdub the hi-hats, cymbals and toms afterwards, on separate tracks. Fills can be left until later too. Having the drums separated like this makes it easier to carry out editing procedures.

Spread the kit

If all the drum parts in a song are on a single track – you've imported a MIDI file perhaps – and some serious editing is required, use the menu function MIDI >

Dissolve Part to unravel them. You'll be presented with a dialogue box asking if you want 'Separate Channels' or 'Separate Pitches'. Choose the latter and each drum sound will be assigned its own track enabling easy cutting and pasting and so on. The original track remains intact, but muted.

Logical Editor tips

Okay, we've reached the chapter you're about to skip over, right? Nothing strikes fear deeper into the heart of the average Cubase user than mention of the Logical Editor, let alone the dreaded Transformer. However, the fear is largely unjustified because they are incredibly useful, powerful features and not at all difficult to understand (well, just a little bit) once you get to know them better. In fact, the Logical Editor becomes easier to understand and simpler to use with each successive version of Cubase that appears. Most MIDI editing is done within the Key and List editors on individual and small groups of events but there are probably times when you wish that you could change a large chunk of data in one fell swoop.

Suppose you need to find all the notes on a track that are between C1 and C3 in pitch, that are 30 ticks long, with a velocity value of between 80 and 100 and then alter all of them to 90 ticks in length with a velocity value of 120 – a tall order, that could take hours in the Key Editor but only minutes using the Logical Editor.

Examine the presets

Basically, this is how it works: You set up 'filter conditions' to find certain events, select 'functions' to perform on those events, followed by the 'actions'. The best way to get to grips with Logical Editor is to examine the factory presets and an easy one to start with is 'Fixed Velocity 100', from 'standard set 1', Figure 13.1.

What you see is:

- Type Is – Equal – Note (the filter condition),
- Transform (the function – top left corner),
- Value 2 – Set to fixed value – 100 (the action),

or in other words, 'Transform all selected notes to a fixed velocity value of 100'.

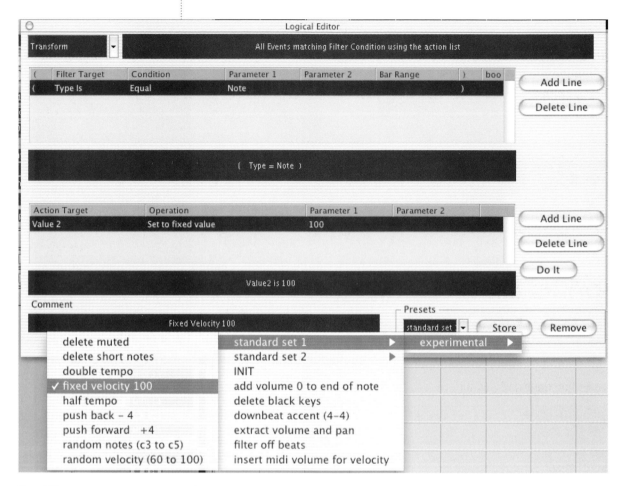

Figure 13.1
The Logical Editor

These presets not only serve as an excellent way to understand how the Logical Editor works but also as templates for use in your own projects. For example, a commonly needed function when polishing a MIDI sequence is randomisation. This can done by modifying the 'random velocity (60 – 100)' preset, Figure 13.2. All you have to do is substitute the preset velocity values with those of your own. This method has an advantage over the Track Parameter 'Random' feature because you can select a group of notes rather than the whole track and it's quicker than the Merge MIDI in Loop function.

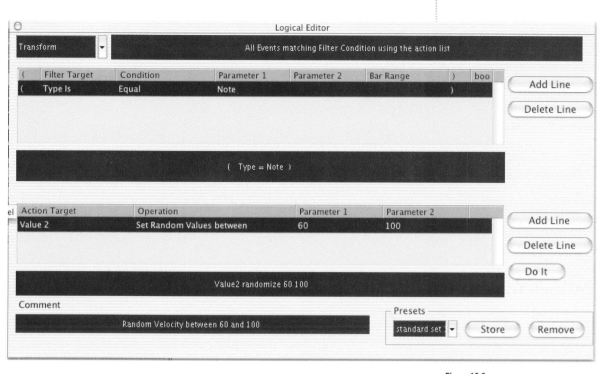

Figure 13.2
Use the Logical Editor presets as templates

Preset functions and tips on use

Here's a run-down on the Logical Editor factory presets and a few tips on using them.

Standard set 1

- Delete muted – Deletes all muted notes in a selected group. However if no particular notes are selected the muted one are deleted one at a time, in reverse order. A useful function for removing muted notes that would otherwise remain displayed when printing a score .
- Delete short notes – Deletes all notes shorter than the specified length. A default setting of 20 can be modified. This is useful if you need to delete short, mistakenly played notes.
- Fixed velocity 100 – Sets all the velocities to 100. Modify the value to suit.
- Double tempo – Repositions events (divides by two) to mimic a double tempo. Do it repeatedly for quadrupled time and so on. Useful as an alternative to modifying the Tempo Track or having different tracks playback in different tempos.
- Push back – 4 – Moves all events 4 ticks later in the project. Do it repeatedly to move them further. Handy when tracks have been duplicated to playback different sounds and you don't want their events (particularly the notes) having exactly the same starting points.
- Push forward +4 – Moves all the events 4 ticks later in the project.
- Random notes (C3 – C5) – Randomises all notes to positions between C3 and C5. Useful for turning perfectly good tunes into unintelligible rubbish.

- Random velocity (60 – 100) – Randomises note velocity values between 60 and 100. Of course, you can modify this to suit your project. Useful for 'humanising' fixed velocity notes that were 'painted' in the Key Editor or inserted with Step Input.

Standard set 2

- Del patch changes – Deletes Program changes and Bankselect messages. Useful if you change your mind, I suppose.
- Del velocity below 30, 35, 40 and 45 – Four separate presets that delete notes with velocity values below the set threshold. Useful for deleting accidentally played notes with low velocity values.
- Del.aftertouch – Deletes all Aftertouch/Channel Pressure messages. Useful when exporting MIDI files for use on older synthesisers that do not recognise Aftertouch messages.
- Extract note (C3 60) – Extracts the note C3 and moves them to a new part on a new MIDI track. Modify it to extract notes of your choice. Useful when you need to extract something like a snare from a drum track, for editing or effects treatment.
- High notes to channel 1 – The default setting transforms notes above C3 to channel 1. For example – a note such as E3 on channel 2 will be transformed into E3 on channel 1. Useful for outputting certain notes to different channels, to play back different instruments within one part. To do this ensure that the channel output in the Inspector is set to ANY. Of course, you can modify these settings to whatever suits you.
- Low notes to channel 2 – Works on the same principle as above, only this time the default setting transforms notes below C3 to channel 2.
- Set notes to fixed pitch C3 – Presumably does what it says. However my version of SX displays the message 'Preset is invalid!' and proceeds to crash my computer!

Main menu

- INIT – Initialises the Logical Editor.
- Add volume 0 to end of note – Inserts a Controller value (default is No.11, Volume) at the end of a note(s).
- Delete black keys – Does exactly that.
- Downbeat accent (4 – 4) – The default setting adds a velocity value of 30 to all four down beats in a bar of 4/4. This is useful for stressing certain beats in music that has been entered manually with a mouse or via Step Input. Modify the settings to suit your own music.
- Extract volume and pan – Controllers No.11, Volume and No. 10 Pan, are extracted from the track and inserted in a new part on another track. If you replace 'Extract' with 'Copy' as the function, the data will be pasted to a new part on a new track. The duplicated volume and pan data can now be shared with other tracks by copying and pasting.
- Filter offbeats – Deletes any note not on the beat.
- Insert midi volume for velocity – Presumably does what it says. However my

version of SX displays the message 'Preset is invalid!' and proceeds to crash my computer!

Share your knowledge

You can store Logical Editor presets as individual files within the Cubase program folder. Go to the Presets > Logical Edit sub folder. You can't edit the files here but you can reorganise them into sub folders and so on. Doing this makes it it easier to share your presets with other Cubase SX/SL users. Just copy the files and pass them on.

Bass notes to kick drum

Here's a neat time saving trick . You've recorded a simple bass part and you want a kick drum to shadow it, a beat for every note. This is what you do:

1 Select the bass part in the Project window and use the MIDI menu to open the Logical Editor.
2 Choose 'Copy' as the function (top left).
3 If necessary, change the line in the 'filter' section to read: Type Is (Filter Target) Equal (Condition) Note (Parameter).
4 Change the line in the 'actions' section to read: Value 1 (Action Target) Set to fixed value (Operation) C1 (Parameter 1)
5 Press 'Do It'.

Figure 13.3
'Copy all notes and fix their value to C1' - a new preset

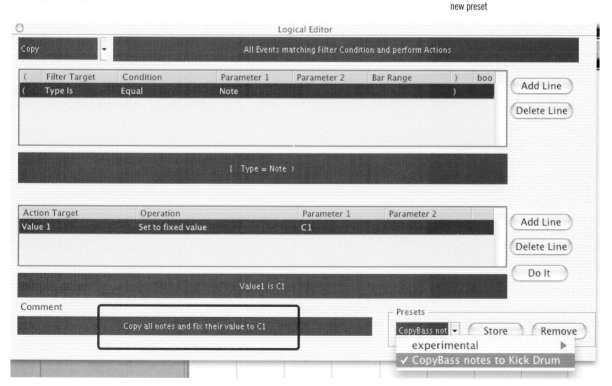

Figure 13.4
Bass notes duplicated as kick drum beats

A new part will be created on a new track containing a string of kick drum notes (in this case C1) that follow the bass part note for note. All the velocity values are copied too. We can sum up the whole operation as Copy all notes and fix their value to C1 (the kick drum) Figures 13.3 and 13.4.

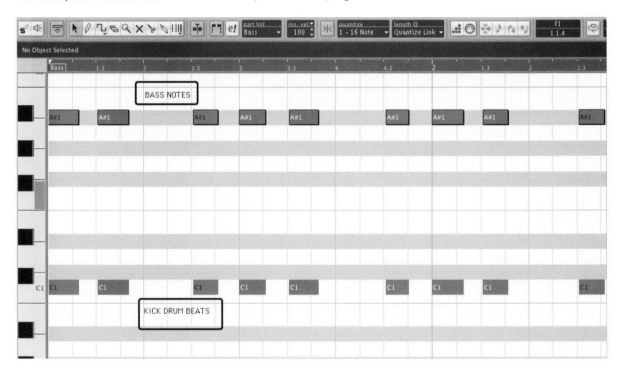

No comment?

You may like to add a comment or two about any presets you make in the Comment field (near the bottom of the Logical Editor), particularly if they are complicated. Info that you type here will be stored along with the preset itself.

Audio tips

Stretch fit

When you import an audio file it doesn't always fit exactly to bar lengths and using the Repeat function to create loops will often leave small, audible gaps between the parts. Time stretching them first, with the arrow tool, will make them easier to repeat seamlessly.

First, make sure that Sizing Applies Time Stretch is selected for the Arrow tool and that Snap is turned on and set to Grid/Bar. All you have to do is select the audio event, grab the handles and stretch it as far as the next bar. Once stretched, you can use the Repeat function to loop the audio.

Before you use the Time Stretch tool, make sure that it's using the correct algorithm for the job. There are five available in the Preferences (Time Stretch Tool page) – Mode 1, Mode 2, Advanced, MPEX and Drum. The quality improves from Mode 1 through to MPEX. The Drum mode has been optimised for rhythmic material, Figure 14.1.

Figure 14.1
You can stretch audio quickly with the Time Stretch tool

Regions

Regions are useful – extremely useful in fact. You can create regions easily by selecting audio with the Range Selection tool in the Sample Editor and clicking on the Add Region button, Figure 14.2.

Once a region is created you can:

- Name it
- Drag it into the Project window using the mouse, to create a new event
- Select it in the list and apply processing
- Select it in the list and audition it, using the Play Region button
- Select it in the Pool and use 'Bounce Selection' to create a new audio file.

Info

As well as using the Time Stretch Tool, you can use the Time Stretch dialogue for more control over the process (Audio > Process > Time Stretch).

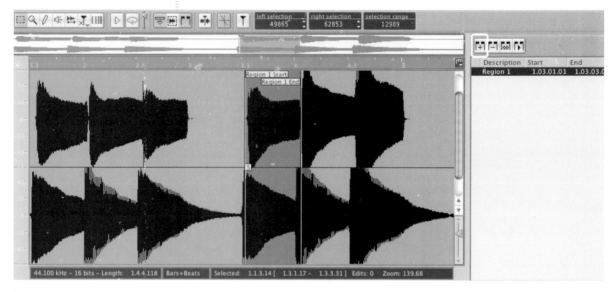

Figure 14.2
Creating regions

Instant harmonies

Here's a trick for creating quick harmonies on vocals and monophonic instrument lines. Try this example:

• Record a few bars of singing, single note guitar or another instrument. Select the recorded audio event and drag a copy to the track above. Open the Pitch Shift dialogue (Audio > Process > Pitch Shift). Transpose the event up a fourth (5 semitones).
• Return to the original event and drag another copy to the track below, open the Pitch Shift dialogue and this time transpose the new event down a fifth (7 semitones).
• Now play all three tracks together. Instant harmonies! The trick works well with instruments like saxophone. For instance, an alto sax line can be used to create a soprano sax line above and a tenor sax or baritone sax line below. Of course it works best over a fairly static chord sequence.

It isn't normal

If you've accidentally recorded some audio at too low a level and it's impossible to re-record it, the Normalizing feature (Audio > Process > Normalize) will probably get you out of trouble, Figure 14.3.

After selecting the event, you set a maximum level for the audio. Cubase will analyse the audio and determine its highest level, subtract it from the level you have set and then raise everything by that amount. If you want it to be as loud as

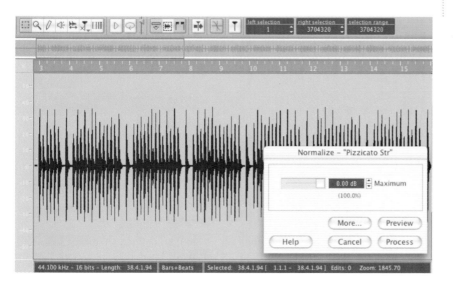

Figure 14.3
Audio before using Normalize

possible just leave it at 0.00 (100%). Use the Preview button and listen carefully because normalizing an audio signal will raise the noise level, particularly in the quiet bits, Figure 14.4.

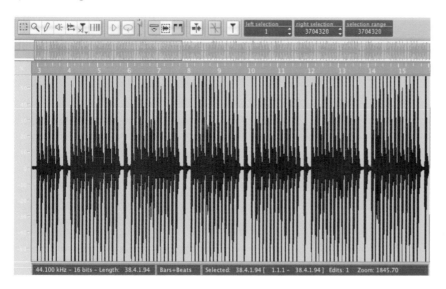

Figure 14.4
Audio after using Normalize

Detect Silence

As mentioned above, background noise on a recording can be a problem, particularly on material with lots of gaps in-between notes such as vocals or instrumental solos. The problem can usually be solved with Noise Gate, found on the Audio

Processing menu, Figure 14.5. Basically, you set a specified threshold level and Noise Gate scans the audio for sections with weaker levels and replaces them with silence. It works well but on long clips it can be time consuming checking the results with the Preview function.

Figure 14.5
Noise Gate looks for weaker audio levels and replaces them with silence.

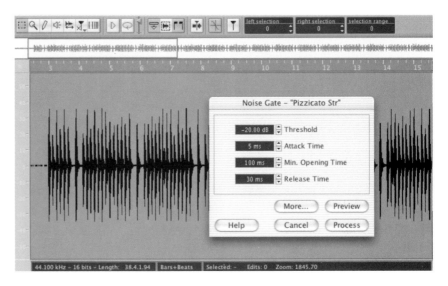

One way of dealing with background noise is to use the Detect Silence feature. Because you can see the waveform changes actually taking place, generally speaking, you have more control, Figure 14.6.

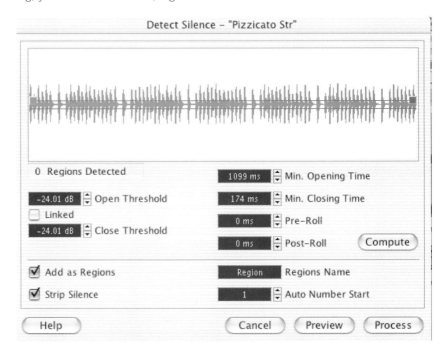

Figure 14.6
Audio file before using computing with Detect Silence

Unlike Noise Gate, which actually processes the audio, Detect Silence searches for silent sections in an event and does one of two things – splits the event, removing the silent parts altogether, or creates regions related to the non-silent sections. This way, background noise can be eliminated without altering the audio signal itself. As a rule of thumb, low threshold settings will yield good results on material with frequent gaps – vocals and so on.

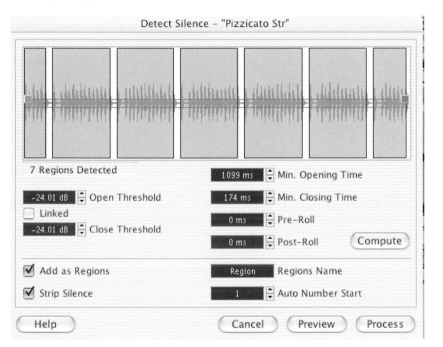

Figure 14.7
Audio file after computing with Detect Silence

Creative silence

As mentioned above, regions can be incredibly useful. Here's a few of the things you can do when you create regions in conjunction with the Detect Silence feature:

- Manipulating speech – You've recorded a section of speech, perhaps as part of a jingle but you need to rearrange some of the words or sentences. After creating the regions you can shuffle the speech segments around to your heart's content.
- Optimising synchronisation – If you're using time code to link with an external recording device you may experience a slight drift between MIDI and audio material, particularly if it's a long sequence. One way round the problem is to create several shorter audio sequences – the more the merrier. You'll get more trigger points between MIDI and audio events.
- ReCycle style drum loops – You can use Detect Silence as an alternative to Hitpoints for slicing up drum loops into small segments. They can subsequently be treated in same way as MIDI events – sped up and slowed down, just like REX files.

Reinventing history

If you apply processing to an audio clip and later decide that you don't like it you can use the Offline Process History dialogue to remove it – even if it's in the middle of the history, Figure 14.8. Not only can you remove processing, you can also modify it. For example – you have used the Distortion plug-in on an audio clip but the setting's not quite right. Select the clip and find the Distortion processing in the history and use the 'Modify' function to get it just how you want it.

Figure 14,8
You can remove and modify previously processed audio with Offline Process History

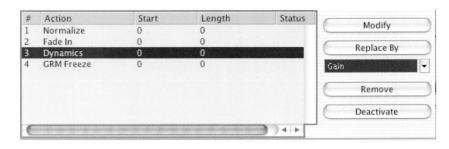

Cut and paste

If you make your own loops it's quite likely that you will want to mix bits from one audio file with another. You can do this by cutting and pasting audio from one file to another, using the Merge Clipboard function, found in the Audio Processing menu.

First select all or part of audio file 'A' in the Sample Editor and save it to the clipboard using Ctrl+C (on the Mac, Command +C). Close the Sample Editor and in the Project window, select audio file 'B' and use Merge Clipboard to paste 'A' across. The audio is pasted at the beginning of the selection. Before you complete the process, use the Preview button to listen to the mix and adjust the balance between 'A' and 'B' using the 'Sources mix' slider. Pressing 'More' will give you crossfade options.

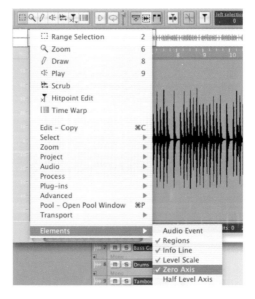

Figure 14.9
Decide what to display in the Sample Editor with the Quick Menu

Use the blue box

Like the Project window the Sample Editor has an overview display. Drag it around to work on specific sections of an audio clip. Stretch it to the left of right to resize it and encompass more audio. Or, most useful of all, use it to zoom in on a specific area by shrinking it.

Zero Crossings

If you do any cutting and pasting of audio in Sample Editor it's advisable to activate the Snap to Zero Crossing button to avoid nasty pops and clicks. They happen as a result of two juxtaposed signals, each with different volume levels. To avoid the problem when editing in the Project window you'll need to tick the Snap to Zero Crossing box in the Preferences (Editing > Audio page).

Info

You can choose what to show and hide in the Pool using the View field.

Inserting audio clips into a Project

You can insert audio clips directly into a project from the Pool. Scroll the Project cursor to the position you want the clip to go, select the clip and use Pool > Insert into Project > At Cursor to insert it. A quicker way to do it – first alter the clip's position in the Origin Time column and use Pool > Insert into Project > At Origin. This method eliminates the need to go into the Project window and alter the Project cursor manually.

Quick tip

Hold down Shift to select more than one clip at a time as you select them.

Crowded Pool

Large projects usually result in a crowded Pool. Tidy things up by putting different types of audio clips into different folders using Create Folder found on the Pool menu. However you can't place audio clips in a video folder and vice versa, Figure 14.10.

Figure 14.10
Get organised and create folders in the Pool

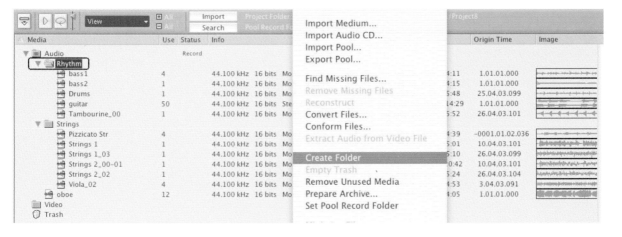

Quick tip

To sort clips in the Pool by name or date, click on the arrow, in the selected column heading. Click again to switch between ascending and descending order.

Pool cleaning

If the Pool becomes cluttered with unused files you can remove them using Pool > Remove Unused Media. You'll be asked whether you want to remove them from the hard disk altogether or put them in the Pool Trash folder. Unless you're sure that you'll never need them again, either later in the project or for a different project altogether, put them in the Trash folder to be on the safe side.

Missing files

It's not a good idea to rename or move audio files outside of Cubase. Cubase will consider them missing. When you next open the project Cubase will ask you whether you want to locate them yourself or let Cubase try to find them for you. Ignore the dialogue if you wish and choose 'Close'. The project will still open, but without the missing files, which will be indicated by question marks in the Status column, in the Pool.

If you've just moved the files you can probably locate them using Find Missing Files... found on the Pool menu. If you've renamed them it might not be quite so easy, particularly if you can't remember their new names. But if you do remember their names, use the Search function to find them (opened by clicking on the Search button, on the Toolbar).

Reconstruction work

Normally, if you delete a file from the hard disk, you can't get it back. But, if you accidentally deleted a file that you've processed at some point in the project you may be able to bring it back from beyond the grave. Open the Pool and with any luck the file will be marked 'Reconstructible'. Select the clip and use Reconstruct (Pool menu) to rebuild it.

Quantize tips

Which Quantize value?

Cubase provides plenty of scope for quantizing. Use the Quantize Selector, in either the Project window or any of the MIDI editors, to select a quantize option. However, the various options, what they do and when to use them can be confusing to the uninitiated. There are two main types:

- Over Quantize – use this type of quantizing to move all the notes played to the nearest division of the beat. For example, select 1/8 Note to move everything to the nearest eighth note, 1/16 to the nearest sixteenth note and so on. The musical result of course will be dead straight. Use it to correct inaccurate playing and when you need a straight feel – electro or classical music perhaps.
- Iterative Quantize – use this type of quantizing to move the notes towards the closest quantize value. Define how far the notes are moved, and what is considered already close to the Quantize value using the 'Iterative Strength' and 'Non Quantize' values in the Quantize Setup dialogue Figure 15.1. An

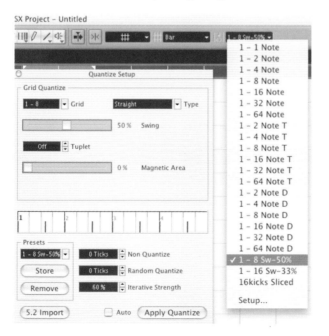

Figure 15.1
Settings made in the Quantize Setup are reflected in the pop-up menus

Quick tip

Press Q on the computer keyboard to apply Over Quantize

Iterative Strength of 60% is the default setting, and works well as an all rounder. The musical result of this type of quantizing is less rigid than Over Quantize and you can apply it progressively, as needed. In other words, if you record a passage, and after applying Iterative Quantize it's still not tight enough, just apply it again. Of course, you can only do this so many times before everything ends up dead straight, which completely defeats the purpose. Use it to correct your playing without loosing too much feel.

Home grown grooves

Over and Iterative quantisation is fine for many uses but if you want to make your own grooves you can further adjust the values in the Quantize Setup dialogue, Figure 15.1. Here's a quick run-down of the main functions:

- Grid value and Type – where you select basic note values for quantizing. Using these menus amounts to the same thing as using the Quantize Selector on the Toolbar, in the Project window.
- The Swing Slider – adjust this slider to create a swing or shuffle feel by offsetting every second note on the Grid.
- Magnetic Area – where only specified notes, within a certain distance from the grid, are affected. Use the slider and percentage values to define the area.

The beauty of this set-up box is that you can hear the results very quickly using the Apply button. The box remains open ready for further changes. Even better, if you tick the Auto box the changes are heard in real time, as you move the sliders. All very intuitive. When you've found the exact setting for the job, save it as a preset ready for further use. It will then show up on the Quantize Selector pop-up menu whenever you need it.

'A' levels

There are a four more quantize features to be found in the MIDI menu under Advanced Quantize. Here's what they do:

- Quantize Lengths – Use this function to quantize a note's length without actually moving it. Set the quantize value in the Length Quantize pop-up menu in any MIDI Editor's toolbar. Why would you need this? Well, it has its uses. For example, you may have played a series of organ chords, one chord per bar for several bars. The notes in each chord are unlikely to be all the same length. After initially quantizing their start positions you could then quantize their lengths to make them sound even.
- Quantize Ends – this is a bit like Over Quantize in reverse. Only the ends of the notes are quantised, according to the value that you select in the pop-up menu.
- Undo Quantize – does exactly that. It's independent of the regular Undo History.
- Freeze Quantize – use this to make the quantizing permanent. You can then re-quantize the notes again if you wish. This function cannot be undone.

Grooves to go

If you're using version 2 you'll find a fifth function on the Advanced Quantize menu, not included with version 1 – Part to Groove. You can use this to extract grooves from MIDI material. Just select a MIDI part and apply. The resulting groove will be added to the existing Quantize menu, ready for further use.

Quantizer – the plug-in

There's usually more than one way to carry out a task in Cubase and quantizing is no exception. If you want to try out different grooves on a track and don't yet want to commit, use the Quantizer plug-in as a track parameter Insert, Figure 15.2. It does pretty much the same as the normal quantize functions but there's one big difference – you can experiment as much as you need whilst listening to the results as you apply them. Some of the more advanced features are missing though. However, it does contains a unique feature of its own called Delay.

Automating the Quantizer

You can apply a whole string of quantize values to a single track by using the Quantizer plug-in as an Insert and using track automation. Here's an example:

1 In the Project window, select a Quantize vale of 1/8 Note, turn on Snap and set the Locators to encompass a single bar.
2 Between the Locators, double click on a MIDI track to create an empty part and set the track output to play back a bass sound of some kind.
3 Select the part and use Ctrl+E (on the Mac, Command+E) to open the Key Editor and with Pencil tool enter this simple bass pattern, Figures 15.3 and 15.4. Use a Length Quantize value of 1/16 Note.

Figure 15.2
Use the Quantizer plug-in as a track parameter Insert

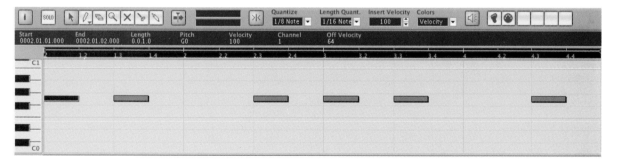

Figures 15.3 and 15.4
A simple bass pattern

4 Play it back. If necessary, turn Snap off and lengthen the notes slightly.
5 Return to the Project window and use the Repeat function to copy the part 15 times, Figure 15.5.

Figure 15.5
Use the Repeat function for multiple repeats

Figure 15.6 (far right)
Set up the Quantizer plug-in

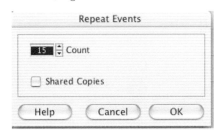

6 Set up the Quantizer plug-in as an Insert on the track, Figure 15.6. Set a value of '8' as the Quantize Note parameter.
7 Open the automation track (click on the '+' tab) and find the 'Swing Ins 1' parameter in the pop-up menu. If it's not there choose 'More...' and add it to the menu.
8 Now, with the Pencil tool, enter nodes at one or two bar intervals or draw a ramp, progressively raising the swing value, Figure 15.7. Play the track to hear the changes.

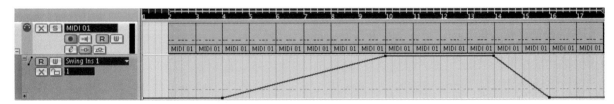

Figure 15.7
Automating the Quantizer swing values

Experiment further by automating the other Quantize parameters on automation sub tracks. For more automation tips see chapter 17.

Automatic Quantize

Not to be confused with automation. You can use this handy function to automatically quantize events as you play them. Activate the AQ button on the Transport panel before you record a part. The part will be played back already quantised. This is useful if you know in advance that a certain quantize setting is going to work.

Loops and hitpoints

As a direct result of programs like Cubase much of the music we hear today includes audio loops. Hip-hop, house and trance music producers, of course, use loops extensively and even rock bands are now incorporating them into their tracks. Film composers too are using loops alongside conventional orchestras.

To use loops effectively with Cubase you need to know how to work with Hitpoints, a special feature of the Sample Editor. It works best on drums and other rhythmic material and detects attack transients (rhythmic hits) in an audio file and marks them as 'hitpoints'. Once you've created the hitpoints, you can perform all kinds of wizardry on audio files such as making them fit the tempo of a song or even change a song's tempo whilst retaining the timing of a drum loop. In other words, you can work with audio material in the same way as you do with MIDI material.

Creating hitpoints

You're all fired up because you've found a great drum loop and you can't wait to get started on building a song around it. Trouble is, you don't know the original tempo of the drum loop. You have a rough idea but it could take hours to nail down the exact bpm. No problem. Use the hitpoint feature to calculate the tempo quickly.

Select the drum loop and use 'Locators to Selection' to encompass it. Now double-click on the loop to open it in the Sample Editor. What you do next depends on whether you're using version 1 or 2.

In version 1, you'll need to define a section of the loop with a complete number of bars and audition the loop, all the while listening carefully to the tempo (the loop's not Cubase's). If necessary, trim the audio event with the event start and end points. In many cases only the end point will need adjusting.

When the audio loops seamlessly, click the Hitpoint Mode button, and the hitpoints will appear at the beginning of each sound in the loop, Figure 16.1. Enter the length of the loop in the Bars and Beats field, check that the time signature is set correctly and the real tempo of the loop will be displayed in the Original Tempo display.

In version 2 the process has been automated and is much more accurate. If you need to make a selection use the Range tool. Otherwise just click the Hitpoint Mode button and use the Hitpoints Detection dialogue, Figure 16.2. Leave the 'Use level scan' and 'Adjust Loop' boxes ticked and enter values in the 'Maximum bars' and 'Beats' fields. Make an intelligent guess as to the loop's likely minimum

Figure 16.1
Hitpoints calculated in SX 1

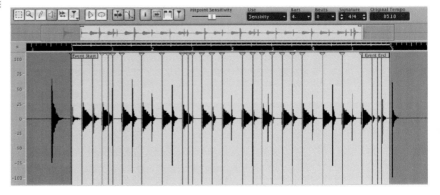

and maximum tempo values and enter them in the appropriate boxes. Cubase is pretty dammed good at calculating the tempo but the more accurate you are, the better the result.

Figure 16.2
The Hitpoints Detection dialogue

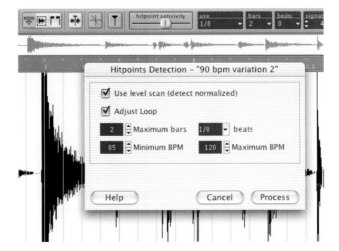

Click Process and the hitpoints are calculated. Your loop is shown in the ruler and the original tempo is shown on the toolbar.

Slicing and dicing

After you've created hitpoints for a drum loop you can make it follow the project's tempo. In fact by chopping the file into slices it will play back at any speed you fancy (within reason).

Basically you need one 'hit' per slice so gradually move the Sensitivity Slider to the left or right until you've achieved the desired effect. Then slice them for real using Create Audio Slices from the Audio menu. The Sample Editor closes and the loop is sliced at each hitpoint. The event in the Project window is replaced by an audio part containing the slices and the loop is automatically set to the Cubase tempo, Figure 16.3. That's pretty neat but the real clever bit is that it will playback at any tempo you choose.

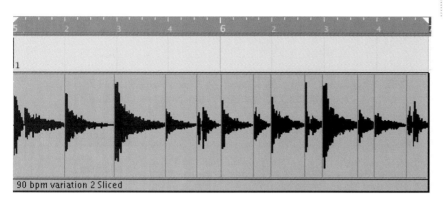

Figure 16.3
Sliced audio will play back at any tempo

Mind the gap

When playing back sliced audio at a tempo lower than the loop's original tempo, there might be audible gaps between the slices, Figure 16.4. Select the slices in the Audio Part Editor and use 'Close Gaps' from the Audio menu to stretch them to size. Before doing so make sure that 'Always use Drum Mode for Close Gaps' is checked in the Preferences (Time Stretch Tool page).

> **Quick tip**
>
> Hiding unwanted 'double-hits' is not always possible using just the Sensitivity Slider and further editing is needed. Zoom in on a segment and use the Pencil tool to divide them further.

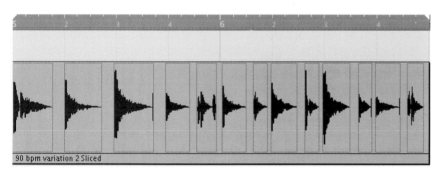

Figure 16.4
Gaps appear between audio slices when they are played at slower tempos

Seven ways to edit hitpoints

- Setting the sensitivity - use the Sensitivity slider to increase or reduce the number of hitpoints. As a rule, always try this method first.
- Setting hitpoints according to note values - use the drop-down menu on the Sample Edit toolbar. Note values are selected and only hitpoints close to the selected value are used. The correct length of the loop must be set in the Bars and Beats field in the toolbar along with the time signature, Figure 16.5.
- Disabling slices - use the Hitpoint Edit tool, Figure 16.6. In Disable mode the cursor changes to a cross. Clicking on the hitpoint's triangle disables the hitpoint itself. This is handy if you have too many hitpoints.

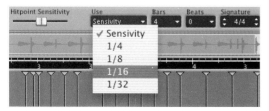

Figure 16.5 (left)
Hitpoints to note values

Figure 16.6 (right)
Disabling slices

- Locking slices - use the Hitpoint Edit tool in Lock mode. Use this when you have "double hits" in one or several slices and increasing the sensitivity adds unwanted extra slices.
- Setting hitpoints manually - use the Pencil tool to add missing slices.
- Moving hitpoints - use the Hitpoint Edit tool after manual editing. This might be needed if you have placed a hitpoint too far away from the start of a sound or in the sound itself.
- Deleting hitpoints - use the Hitpoint Edit tool in Move mode to drag a hitpoint from the Sample Edit window.

Try these

Once you've created audio slices you can create all kinds of unusual effects by experimenting with the individual segments. Try muting slices with the Mute tool or changing their order, to create a completely new drum pattern. What about treating them with effects and EQ? High-hats sound great when treated with the Metalizer plug-in, Figure 16.7. What about using Reverb A on individual snare hits? You might need to raise the volume of a quiet hi-hat with Gain (Audio menu). Over to you...

Figure 16.7
High-hats sound great when treated with the Metalizer plug-in

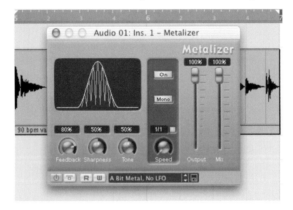

Looping and grooving

You can quantize audio loops after they've been sliced in Cubase in the same way that you quantize MIDI material. In the Project window, double-click the loop to open the Audio Part Editor and open the Quantize Setup box, from the MIDI menu. Okay, off you go!

Feeling groovy

You've found a drum loop that was played with a particularly great 'feel'. You're using it as the basis for a new project and you want to project that 'feel' onto the MIDI tracks. Can it be done? Yes – but first you'll have to create a groove quantize map.

First, create hitpoints for the loop in the Sample Editor (see above). Now extract the groove using Create Groove Quantize, found in the Audio menu. Pull down the Quantize pop-up, in the Project window, and you'll find an additional item at the bottom of the list, with the same name as the file from which you extracted the groove. Now you can apply that drummer's feel onto other MIDI and audio drum loops.

Appendix 1 – Default key commands

We've all seen them in the movies. Those people who never use a mouse when working with a computer. Their fingers fly like magic over the keyboard as they hack into the Bank of England or MI6 main frame computer.

You can work just as fast with Cubase SX/SL if you get to know the default key commands. If you use Cubase regularly, it's a good idea to learn one or two new key commands each day. Most are logical and easy to remember.

You can add your own key commands using the Key Commands window (File > Key Commands…) and even alter the existing default set (although there seems little point in doing so).

Keep this list by you as you work. Your mouse will soon become redundant!

Audio category

Option	PC Key command	Mac Key command
Adjust Fades to Range	A	A
Crossfade	X	X
Find Selected in Pool	Ctrl+F	Command+F

Devices category

Option	PC Key command	Mac Key command
Mixer	F3	F3
Video	F8	F8
VST Connections	F4	F4
VST Instruments	F11	F12

Edit category

Option	PC Key command	Mac Key command
Autoscroll	F	F
Copy	Ctrl+C	Command+C
Cut	Ctrl+X	Command+X
Cut Time	Ctrl+Shift+X	Command+Shift+X
Delete	Del or Back	Del or Back
Delete Time	Shift+Back	Shift+Back
Duplicate	Ctrl+D	Command+D
Group	Ctrl+G	Command+G
Insert Silence	Ctrl+Shift+E	Command+Shift+E
Left Selection Side to Cursor	E	E
Lock	Ctrl+Shift+L	Command+Shift+L

Edit category (contd)

Option	PC Key command	Mac Key command
Move Insert Cursor to Part Start	0	0
Move to Cursor	Ctrl+L	Command+L
Mute	M	M
Mute Events	Shift+M	Shift+M
Mute/Unmute Objects	Alt+M	Option+M
Open Default Editor	Ctrl+E	Command+E
Open Score Editor	Ctrl+R	Command+R
Open/Close Editor	Return	Return
Paste	Ctrl+V	Command+V
Paste at Origin	Alt+V	Option+V
Paste Time	Ctrl+Shift+V	Command+Shift+V
Record Enable	R	R
Redo	Ctrl+Shift+Z	Command+Shift+Z
Repeat	Ctrl+K	Command+K
Right Selection Side to Cursor	D	D
Select All	Ctrl+A	Command+A
Select None	Ctrl+Shift+A	Command+Shift+A
Snap On/Off	J	J
Solo	S	S
Split At Cursor	Alt+X	Option+X
Split Range	Shift+X	Shift+X
Undo	Ctrl+Z	Command+Z
Ungroup	Ctrl+U	Command+U
Unlock	Ctrl+Shift+U	Command+Shift+U
Unmute Objects	Shift+U	Shift+U

Devices category

Option	PC Key command	Mac Key command
Mixer	F3	F3
Video	F8	F8
VST Connections	F4	F4
VST Instruments	F11	F12

Edit category

Option	PC Key command	Mac Key command
Autoscroll	F	F
Copy	Ctrl+C	Command+C
Cut	Ctrl+X	Command+X
Cut Time	Ctrl+Shift+X	Command+Shift+X
Delete	Del or Back	Del or Back
Delete Time	Shift+Back	Shift+Back
Duplicate	Ctrl+D	Command+D
Group	Ctrl+G	Command+G
Insert Silence	Ctrl+Shift+E	Command+Shift+E
Left Selection Side to Cursor	E	E
Lock	Ctrl+Shift+L	Command+Shift+L
Move Insert Cursor to Part Start	0	0
Move to Cursor	Ctrl+L	Command+L
Mute	M	M
Mute Events	Shift+M	Shift+M
Mute/Unmute Objects	Alt+M	Option+M
Open Default Editor	Ctrl+E	Command+E
Open Score Editor	Ctrl+R	Command+R
Open/Close Editor	Return	Return
Paste	Ctrl+V	Command+V
Paste at Origin	Alt+V	Option+V
Paste Time	Ctrl+Shift+V	Command+Shift+V
Record Enable	R	R
Redo	Ctrl+Shift+Z	Command+Shift+Z
Repeat	Ctrl+K	Command+K
Right Selection Side to Cursor	D	D
Select All	Ctrl+A	Command+A
Select None	Ctrl+Shift+A	Command+Shift+A
Snap On/Off	J	J
Solo	S	S
Split At Cursor	Alt+X	Option+X
Split Range	Shift+X	Shift+X
Undo	Ctrl+Z	Command+Z
Ungroup	Ctrl+U	Command+U
Unlock	Ctrl+Shift+U	Command+Shift+U
Unmute Objects	Shift+U	Shift+U

Editors category

Option	PC Key command	Mac Key command
Show/Hide Infoview	Ctrl+I	Command+I
Show/Hide Inspector	Alt+I	Option+I
Show/Hide Overview	Alt+O	Option+O

File category

Option	PC Key command	Mac Key command
Close	Ctrl+W	Command+W
New	Ctrl+N	Command+N
Open	Ctrl+O	Command+O
Quit	Ctrl+Q	Command+Q
Save	Ctrl+S	Command+S
Save As	Ctrl+Shift+S	Command+Shift+S
Save New Version	Ctrl+Alt+S	Command+Option+S

MIDI category

Option	PC Key command	Mac Key command
Quantize	Q	Q

Navigate category

Option	PC Key command	Mac Key command
Expand/Undo selection in the Project window to the bottom	Shift+Down Arrow	Shift+Down Arrow
Move selected event in the Key Editor down 1 octave	Shift+Down Arrow	Shift+Down Arrow
Expand/Undo selection in the Project window/Key Editor to the left	Shift+Left Arrow	Shift+Left Arrow
Expand/Undo selection in the Project window/Key Editor to the right	Shift+Right Arrow	Shift+Right Arrow
Expand/Undo selection in the Project window to the top	Shift+Up Arrow	Shift+Up Arrow
Move selected event in the Key Editor up 1 octave	Shift+Up Arrow	Shift+Up Arrow
Select next in the Project window (Down)	Down Arrow	Down Arrow
Move selected event in the Key Editor 1 semitone down	Down Arrow	Down Arrow
Select next in the Project window/Key Editor (Left)	Left Arrow	Left Arrow
Select next in the Project window/Key Editor (Right)	Right Arrow	Right Arrow
Select next in the Project window (Up)	Up Arrow	Up Arrow
Move selected event in the Key Editor 1 semitone up	Up Arrow	Up Arrow

Nudge category

Option	PC Key command	Mac Key command
End Left	Alt+Shift+Left Arrow	Option+Shift+Left Arrow
End Right	Alt+Shift+Right Arrow	Option+Shift+Right Arrow
Left	Ctrl+Left Arrow	Ctrl+Left Arrow
Right	Ctrl+Right Arrow	Command+Right Arrow
Start Left	Alt+Left Arrow	Option+Left Arrow
Start Right	Alt+Right Arrow	Option+Right Arrow

Project category

Option	PC Key command	Mac Key command
Open Browser	Ctrl + B	Command + B
Open Markers	Ctrl + M	Command + M
Open Tempo Track	Ctrl + T	Command + T
Open Pool	Ctrl + P	Command + P
Setup	Shift + S	Shift + S

Tool category

Option	PC Key command	Mac Key command
Delete tool	5	5
Draw tool	8	8
Glue tool	4	4
Mute tool	7	7
Next Tool	F10	F10
Play tool	9	9
Previous Tool	F9	F9
Range tool	2	2
Select tool	1	1
Split tool	3	3
Zoom tool	6	6

Transport category

Option	PC Key command	Mac Key command
AutoPunch In	I	I
AutoPunch Out	0	0
Cycle	Pad //	Pad /
Fast Forward	Shift + Pad +	Shift + Pad +
Fast Rewind	Shift + Pad −	Shift + Pad −
Forward	Pad +	Pad +
Input Left Locator	Shift + L	Shift + L
Input Position	Shift + P	Shift + P
Input Right Locator	Shift + R	Shift + R
Input Tempo	Shift + T	Shift + T
Insert Marker	Insert	Insert
Locate Next Event	N	N
Locate Next Number	Shift + N	Shift + N
Locate Previous Event	B	B
Locate Previous Marker	Shift + B	Shift + B
Locate Selection	L	L
Locators to Selection	P	P
Loop Selection	Shift + G	Shift + G
Metronome On	C	C
Nudge Down	Ctrl + Pad −	Command + Pad −

Transport category (contd)

Option	PC Key command	Mac Key command
Nudge Up	Ctrl + Pad +	Command + Pad +
Transport Panel	F2	F2
Play Selection Range	Alt + Space	Option + Space
Recall Cycle Marker 1 to 9	Shift + Pad 1 to Pad 9	Shift + Pad 1 to 9
Record	Pad *	Pad *
Retrospective Record	Shift + Pad *	Shift + Pad *
Return to Zero	Pad . or Pad ,	Pad . or Pad ,
Rewind	Pad −	Pad −
Set Left Locator	Ctrl + Pad 1	Command + Pad 1
Set Marker 1	Ctrl + 1	Command + 1
Set Marker 2	Ctrl + 2	Command + 2
Set Marker 3 to 9	Ctrl + 3 to 9	Command 3 to 9
Set Right Locator	Ctrl + Pad 2	Command + Pad 2
start	Enter	Enter
Start/Stop	Space	Space
Stop	Pad 0	Pad 0
Sync Online	T	T
To Left Locator	Pad 1	Pad 1
To Marker 1	Shift + 1	Shift + 1
To Marker 2	Shift + 2	Shift + 2
To Marker 3 to 9	Pad 3 to 9 or Shift + 3 to 9	Pad 3 to 9 or Shift + 3 to 9
To Right Locator	Pad 2	Pad 2

Window Layout category

Option	PC Key command	Mac Key command
Layout 1 to 9	Alt + Pad 1 to 9	Option + Pad 1 to 9
New	Ctrl + Pad 0	Command + Pad 0
Organize	W	W
Recapture	Alt + Pad 0	Option + Pad 0

Zoom category

Option	PC Key command	Mac Key command
Zoom Full	Shift + F	Shift + F
Zoom In	H	H
Zoom In Tracks	Alt + Down Arrow	Option + Down Arrow
Zoom Out	G	G
Zoom Out Tracks	Alt + Up Arrow	Option + Up Arrow
Zoom to Event	Shift + E	Shift + E
Zoom to Selection	Alt + S	Option + S
Zoom Tracks Exclusive	Z or Ctrl + Down Arrow	Z or Command + Down Arrow

Appendix 2 – Tools summary

Here's a list of the main tools used in Cubase SX//SL – the ones you'll find in the 'right click pop-up tool box' plus a few more. Some of them vary from Editor to Editor. Their functions may vary too.

The toolbar in each editor is customisable and other icons and buttons can be added to it using the toolbar Setup (Ctrl click on the toolbar to open).

Project Window

Arrow tool – Use it to select, add, move, duplicate (hold down Alt key – on the Mac, Option key) resize and time stretch events.

The Range tool – Use it to select whole areas of a project, ready for editing. Click tiny arrow for options.

Scissors – Use it to split events.

Glue tube – Use it to glue events together.

Eraser – Use it to remove events.

Magnifying Glass – Click once to zoom in, drag to zoom in on an area. Hold down Ctrl (on the Mac, Command) to zoom out.

Mute tool – Use it to mute and unmute events.

Time Warp tool – Use it to adjust the Tempo track by dragging positions related to tempo to actual positions in time. Click tiny arrow for options.

Pencil – Use it to draw parts on MIDI and audio tracks and draw automation data on subtracks.

Line tool – Use it to draw automation data on subtracks. Click tiny arrow for options.

Speaker – Use it to audition audio events. Click tiny arrow for manual scrub option.

Key, List and Drum Editors

Arrow tool – Use it to select, add, move, duplicate (hold down Alt key – on the Mac, Option key) resize and time stretch events.

Pencil (Key and List Editor only) – Use it to add notes and alter their length. In the Key Editor, use it to create and edit controller. In the List Editor, use it to insert events.

Drumstick (Drum Editor only) – Use to create and delete drum beats.

Line tool (Key and Drum Editor only) – Use it to draw controller data, in the controller lanes. Click tiny arrow for options.

Eraser – Use it to remove events.

Magnifying Glass – Click once to zoom in, drag to zoom in on an area. Hold down
Ctrl (on the Mac, Command) to zoom out.

Mute tool – Use it to mute and unmute events.

Scissors (Key Editor only) – Use it to split events.

Glue tube (Key and List Editor only) – Use it to glue events together.

Time Warp tool (Key and Drum Editors only) – Use it to tempo map freely
recorded MIDI material. Click tiny arrow for options.

Score Editor

Arrow tool – Use it to select, move and duplicate notes and objects (hold down
Alt key – on the Mac, Option key).

Eraser – Use it to remove notes and objects.

Magnifying Glass – Click once to zoom in, drag to zoom in on an area. Hold down
Ctrl (on the Mac, Command) to zoom out.

Note – Use it to insert notes and change their lengths.

Scissors (Key Editor only) – Use it to split tied notes (click on second note).

Glue tube (Key and List Editor only) – Use it to glue notes of the same pitch.

Q – Open Display Quantize box. Select note(s) first.

Hand – Graphic Move tool. Use it to move notes and objects without affecting
playback.

Knife – Use it to divide notes. For example an 1/8 note into two 1/16 notes.

Sample Editor

The Range tool – Use it to select whole sections of an audio.

Magnifying Glass – Click once to zoom in, drag to zoom in on an area. Hold down
Ctrl (on the Mac, Command) to zoom out.

Pencil – Use it to draw in the waveform display.

Speaker tool – Use it to audition audio.

Scrub tool – Use it to manually audition audio.

Hitpoint Edit tool – Use it to disable audio slices. Click tiny arrow for options.

Time Warp tool – Use it to tempo map freely recorded audio.

Audio Part Editor

Arrow tool – Use it to select, add, move, duplicate (hold down Alt key – on the
Mac, Option key) resize and time stretch events. Click tiny arrow for options.

The Range tool – Use it to select whole areas of an audio part, ready for editing.

Magnifying Glass – Click once to zoom in, drag to zoom in on an area. Hold down
Ctrl (on the Mac, Command) to zoom out.

Eraser – Use it to remove audio events.

Scissors – Use it to split audio events.

Mute tool – Use it to mute and unmute audio events.

Speaker tool – Use it to audition audio events.

Scrub tool – Use it to manually audition audio events.

Time Warp tool – Use it to adjust the Tempo track by dragging positions related to
tempo to actual positions in time. Click tiny arrow for options.

Tempo Track

Arrow – Use it to select tempo events. You can also enter tempo events with the Arrow by holding down the Alt key (on the Mac, Option).

Eraser – Use it to delete tempo events.

Magnifying Glass – Click once to zoom in, drag to zoom in on an area. Hold down Ctrl (on the Mac, Command) to zoom out.

Pencil – Use it to draw and edit tempo events on the tempo grid display.

Appendix 3 – Useful contacts

Arbiter Music Technology
UK distributor for Steinberg, Celemony, Native Instruments.
http://www.arbitermt.co.uk
Tel (Sales): +44 020 8970 1909
Tel (Support): +44 020 8970 1924

K-v-R Audio Plug-in Resources
Excellent web site, with up to date news on the development of VSTi, DXi and AU plug-ins. On the menu: News, Forum, Chat, Reviews, Banks/Patches, Tutorials, Newsletter and free VST Instruments to download.
http://www.kvr-vst.com

Harmony Central
Great web site for all things music tech related. Software and hardware product news, reviews, downloads and so on.
www.harmonycentral.com

Synth Zone
Web site for synth players packed with links covering all aspects of music technology. Very well organised.
www.synthzone.com

Newsgroup: alt.steinberg.cubase
Dozens of daily postings. Good place for friendly advice from long term Cubase users.
http://groups.google.com

Cubase FAQ
Before you ask a question at alt.steinberg.cubase, check here because it might be on Laurence Payne's list of Frequently Asked Questions.
www.laurencepayne.co.uk/CubaseFAQ.htm

Audio Forums
Lots of discussion forums including Cubase.
www.audioforums.com

Cubase Webring

A web ring of sites devoted to Cubase

http://d.webring.com

Espace Cubase

French site with a mailing list. English pages.

http://www.espace-cubase.org

Steinberg Knowledge Base

The latest technical information on Cubase SX/SL and other Steinberg products.

http://service.steinberg.net/knowledge_pro.nsf

Cubase Support Forum

Public, moderated discussion forum for registered Cubase users.

http://forum.cubase.net/cgi-bin/cubase.net/Ultimate.cgi

Music Tech Mag

Monthly Cubase tutorial, regular reviews and Cubase related articles.

Subscriptions: +44 0870 444 8468

www.musictechmag.co.uk

Computer Music

Monthly magazine. Features regular tutorials and Cubase related articles.

Online subscriptions: www.computermusic.co.uk

Future Music

As well as a monthly magazine the Future Music web site is a handy place to catch up on news, gear, making music and buying and selling equipment.

www.futuremusic.co.uk

Index

A1 synth, 68
Acoustic guitar, 53
ACPI mode, 2
Advanced Quantize, 138
AIFF files, 10
Appearance page, 8
Applying Legato, 65
Archive, 17
Archiving file cleanup, 17
Arpache 5, 69
ASIO, 2
ASIO Multimedia Setup, 3
Audio clip, 45, 135
Audio event, 45
Audio file, 45
Audio input level, 31
Audio Part Editor, 144
Audio recording, 45
Audio Slices, 142
Audio tips, 129
Auto Fades, 26
Auto Select, 28
Automatic Quantize, 140
Automating the Quantizer, 139
Automation, 41, 44
AutoPan, 69

Backing up, 17
Bagpipes, 54
Bass guitar, 53
Beat Calculator, 78
Bit depth, 11
Brass instruments, 53
Broadcast Wave File, 47
Buffer settings, 3
Buffer sizes, 3
Buffers, 3

Change note-heads, 112
Change stem directions, 112
Changing channels, 39
Channel Settings window, 39
Channel View Set, 41
Channel, 116
Chase Events Filter, 59
Chord recognition feature, 99
Chorder MIDI plug-in, 68
Clean Lengths, 109
Cleanup, 17
Clips, 45
Colors pop-up menu, 91

Colouring tracks and parts, 35
Combine multiple parts, 100
Comment field, 128
Common panel, 40
Controller curves, 98
Controller Lane, 64, 95, 99
Copy events, 28
Core Audio, 2
CPU Usage, 31
Create a split point, 113
Create controller events, 96
Create controller ramps, 96
Create drum maps, 117
Create Images during Record, 57
Create velocity ramps, 95
Creating hitpoints, 141
Cycle Marker, 34
Cycle record mode, 55
Cycle, 55

Default Project, 8
Delete Doubles, 60
Delete notes, 65
Detect Silence, 132
Detect Silence, 133
Devices menu, 11
Dicing, 142
Direct Monitoring, 55
Disk Cache Usage, 31
Display Quantize tool, 110
Dissolve Part, 121
Distortion, 49
Double notes, 60
Doubles, 60
Drag and drop, 28
Drag Delay, 28
Draw controller curves, 96
Draw velocity curves, 95
Drum beats, entering, 120
Drum Editor, 115
Drum Editor toolbar, 119
Drum Map, 116, 120
Drum Map Setup, 117
Drum Solo button, 119
Drum track tips, 115
Drumstick tool, 119
Duplicate events, 28

Edit hitpoints, 143
Edit mode, 106

Edit single note velocities, 95
Enabling tracks for recording, 52
EQ, 51
Event Layer, 111
Events, 45
Expert button, 5
Exporting track, 81
Expression, use of, 96
Extract grooves, 139

File category, 146
File types, 47
Files, 45
Folder Tracks, 26
Foot icon, 93
Frames, 76
Freeze Quantize, 138

G3 and OS X, 2
Gate effect, 98
Global settings, 5
GM, 11
GM Drum map, 116
Grand piano, 54
Grid value and Type, 138
Groove quantize map, 144
Grooves, 138, 139
Group channels, 41, 44
Guitar part, 114

Hide stems, 112
Hiding channels, 40
History, 18, 134
Hitpoint Edit tool, 143

I-note, 116
Importing audio, 17
Importing MIDI files, 35
Importing tempo maps, 81
Independent loop feature, 100
Info line, 22
Initialise Channel button, 41
Input channel, 48
Input levels, 51
Input transformer, 88
Insert audio clips, 135
Insert effects, 51
Insert Velocity, 91
Inserting silence, 30
Inspector tips, 83

Instrument, 116
Internet, 7
Iterative Quantize, 137

Jazz music, 110

Key change, 112
Key commands, 14, 145
    Audio category, 145
    Devices category, 145
    Edit category, 145, 146
    Editors category, 146
    MIDI category, 146
    Navigate category, 146
    Nudge category, 146
    Project category, 147
    Tool category, 147
    Transport category, 147
    Window Layout category, 147
    Zoom category, 147
Key Editor tips, 91

Latency, 3, 54
Length Compression, 89
Length Correction, 63
Linear time base, 76, 78
Link Channels, 40
List Editor, 59, 101
LM-7 drum module, 74
Locator key commands, 31
Lock icon, 25
Logical Editor, 92
    presets, 125
    tips, 123
Loop button, 100
Loops hitpoints, 141

Mac OSX, 2
Magnetic Area, 138
Magneto, 50
Mapping, 79
Marker track, 33
Markers, 31
Mask function, 102
Merge MIDI in Loop, 71
Metronome, 74
Metronome setup, 74
MIDI Control, 42
MIDI Device Manager, 11
MIDI files, 35, 102, 120
MIDI Input button, 95

MIDI plug, 95
MIDI plug-ins, 68
MIDI ports, 12
MIDI recording tips, 59
MIDI Thru, 12
Missing files, 136
Mixer configurations, 41
Mixer key commands, 42
Mixer tips, 37
Modulation, 64
Monitoring, 54
Move notes sideways, 112
Multiple notes, 63
Musical time base, 76
Mute, 116

No Overlap feature, 109
Noise Gate, 132, 131
Normalizing, 130
Note editing, 95
Notepad, 20
Nudge buttons, 33

O-note, 116
Offline Process History, 134
Online help, 7
Organise layouts box, 13
Output, 116
Output channel, 48
Output level, 31
Over Quantize, 137
Overlapping notes, 63, 109

Page mode, 106
Part to Groove, 139
Parts, 35
Patch changes in real time, 87
Pitch, 116
Pitch bend, 64
Platforms, 16
Plug-in delay, 56
Plug-in Information, 16
Polyphony, 66
Pool, 136, 135
Pop screen, 52
Pop-up tool box, 10
Preferences, 7
Presets, 11
Project Browser, 13
Project Cursor, 31
Project Overview, 22
Project Setup, 10
Project window tips, 21
Punch In, 55
Punch in/out, 56

Quantize, 116
    audio loops, 144
    Ends, 138
    Lengths, 138
    Selector, 137
    Setup dialogue, 137
    tips, 137
Quantizer plug-in, 139
Quick Menu, 10

Random settings, 67
Randomisation, 124
Range tool, 29, 30
Ranges, 29
Record Catch Range, 61
Record enable, 52
Record format, 46, 46
Recording
    acoustic bass, 54
    acoustic guitars, 53
    brass, 53
    electric guitars, 53
    grand piano, 54
    strings, 53
    upright piano, 54
    vocals, 52
Red light, 49
Redo, 18
Regions, 129
Remote control device, 12
Renaming events, 36
Renaming parts, 35
Repeating events with the
    Pencil tool, 28
Resolution, 11
Restricting Polyphony, 66
Retrospective Record, 61
Ruler tracks, 23
Ruler, 23

Sample Editor, 134, 135, 144
Sample rate, 10, 46
Saving mixer settings, 39
Scale Transpose, 89
Score,
    selecting chords, 112
    selecting notes, 112
    staff split point, 113
    transposing instruments, 113
Score Editor, Edit mode, 106
Score Editor, Page mode, 107
Score Editor tips, 105
Scrub dial, 32
Selecting 'Delete Notes', 65
Selecting notes of the same
    pitch, 92

Set Note Info box, 112
Set tablature, 112
Set-up bar, 102
Setting the buffer size, 3
Setup Tips, 1
Shortcuts, 21
Show inspector button, 84
Show Part Borders tool, 100
Shuffling events, 26
Shuttle Speed control, 32
Signal routing, 48
Signature display, 74
Silence, 131
Skins, 8
Slicing, 142
Snap Points, 21
Snap to Zero Crossing, 135
Split point field, 113
Stacked recording, 55
Staff Settings, 108 – 110
Staff Settings box, 112
Staircase, 93
Step Designer MIDI plug-in, 70
Step input, 93 – 95, 120
Stretching audio, 77
String ensembles, 53
Swing Slider, 138
Sync Reference, 7
Syncopation, 110
Syncopation box, 110
System Exclusive, 12
System Exclusive data, 19
System Exclusive Editor, 103

Tablature, 114
Tap Tempo option, 79
Tapping, 79
Templates, 9
Tempo mapping, 79, 80
Tempo record slider, 81
Tempo Track, 74, 81
Time and tempo tips, 73
Time base button, 76
Time signature change, 74
Time stretch, 129
Time stretch dialogue, 77
Time stretch tool, 129
Time stretching, 129
Time warp tool, 80
Time Warp tool, 79, 81
Toolbar, 10, 21
Tools, 10
    Audio Part Editor, 149
    Key, List and Drum Editors,
        148
    Project Window, 148

Sample Editor, 149
Score Editor, 149
Tempo Track, 150
Track archive, 19
Track automation, 139
Track Control, 42
Track Control list, 24
Track Control MIDI plug-in, 70
Track key commands, 25
Track Lists, 25, 36
Transformer, 88
Transport panel, 32
Transport panel, 31
Transpose feature, 71
Transposing, 113
Transposing instrument, 113
Transposing parts, 71
Trash folder, 56
True Tape, 49

Undo, 18
Undo Quantize, 138
Universal Sound Module, 62

Velocity, 66
Velocity Compress, 66
Velocity Shift, 66
Video files, 76
Video track, 76
Violin, 53
Virtual Guitarist plug-in, 95
vmx, 39
Vocal mics, 52
VST Channel window, 38
VST Connections window, 45
VST Inputs window, 52
VST Multitrack page, 3

Wave files, 10
Waveform images, 57
Window layouts, 13
Windows 2000 and XP, 2
Windows 98, 2
Windows and Mac compatibili-
    ty, 16
Windows dialogue, 13
Windows install XP, 2

XG, 11

Zero Crossings, 135
Zoom menu, 34
Zoom options, 24